Professor Johnson
1106 Campus Way #3
Los Angeles, CA 90007

GREAT LETTERS OF
RECOMMENDATION

P.O. Box 27 Graduate School, USA 05308

Don Osborne   Lilly Chow

INQUARTA Publishing   Irvine, California

Great Letters of Recommendation: How to Get Them. How to Write Them.
Copyright © 2007 by Don Osborne and Lilly Chow

Visit our website at http://www.inquarta.com/publishing

ISBN-13: 978-1-931133-04-3
ISBN-10: 1-931133-04-2

This book is designed to provide information regarding graduate school admissions. However, it is sold with the understanding that the publisher and authors are not engaged in rendering legal, financial, or other professional advice. If legal or other expert advice is required, the services of a competent professional should be sought.

Every effort has been made to make the information in this book as complete and as accurate as possible. However, there may be mistakes, both typographical and in content. Therefore, this text should be used only as a general guide and not as the ultimate source of graduate school admissions advice. Furthermore, this manual contains information on writing and publishing that is current only up to the printing date.

The purpose of this text is to educate and entertain. The authors and INQUARTA Publishing specifically disclaim any liability that is incurred from the use or application of the contents of this book.

This book is dedicated to every teacher and mentor who has ever written a letter of recommendation. Each one is a gift.

For Zoe and Cody
—Lilly

ACKNOWLEDGEMENTS

We are deeply indebted to several individuals for agreeing to share their "horror stories" with us: Guillaume Chanfreau, Hillel Chiel, John Conway, Vinita Dew, Stuart Dryer, Michael Eisen, Steven Goates, Elma Gonzalez, Eric Hudson, Niles Lehman, Jeanne Perry, Jeff Saul, David Snoke and Twombly Vern.

Our gratitude also goes out to the following individuals for contributing their personal advice regarding letters of recommendation: Steve Adler, Carl Akerlof, Andy Anderson, Jon Antilla, David Armstrong, Andrew Belmont, Eric Bittner, Jason Brickner, Paul S. Brookes, Robert Carey, Steve Chu, Betty Ciesla, M. Bonner Denton, Brian Derrick, Heather Desaire, Roy Doi, David Drubin, Walter Englander, Kenneth Ford, Roland A. Giolli, Steven S. Gubser, Michael H. Hecht, Carl Hoff, Roald Hoffmann, Todd Holmes, John Janovy, Jr., Frank W. Judd, Kenneth A.R. Kennedy, Lloyd Knox, Everett Lipman, C. J. Martoff, Craig McClure, Coleen T. Murphy, Heino Nitsche, Monte Pettitt, Dean Roddick, Yves Rubin, Bill Saunders, Frances M. Sladek, Joel Tellinghuisen, Rick Trebino, Rainer Weiss, Mike Welsh and Frank Wilczek.

Special thanks to Kristine Jones and Gregory Weiss.

Lastly, we'd like to express our appreciation to Michelle Liu, Monica Osborne, and Judy Clendenin for their assistance with several of the sample LORs.

TABLE OF CONTENTS

PREFACE

Great Letters of Recommendation is the first comprehensive guide on the subject to be designed for both letter-seekers and letter-writers. Heck, we've even included advice for ghostwriters (letter-seekers who are asked to become their own letter-writers). Each of the respective chapters can be read straight through, but if you're in a hurry, browse the chapter summaries below to locate the section that addresses your specific question or concern.

Advice for Letter Seekers:
How to Get Great Letters of Recommendation

Most people think that the LOR process begins when you start narrowing down the list of professors or supervisors who might have something good to say about you. In our opinion, the real starting point involves the attitude that you bring to the process, so we start you off with a set of guiding principles that will help you approach potential recommenders strategically (**Preamble: How to Deserve a Great Letter of Recommendation**). You'll even find scripts you can use to structure those conversations. Next, we set the record straight on which types of recommenders will do your application more good than harm (**FAQ: Choosing Recommenders**). Following that are instructions on how to put together a comprehensive LOR prep package for your letter-writer, with templates and samples that you can adapt for your own use (**Assembling the LOR Prep Package**). Finally, we'll walk you through the more bureaucratic aspects of the LOR—from helping you make an educated decision about confidentiality to discussing the pros and cons of campus letter services, online credential services, and pre-professional committees (**FAQ: Waivers and Logistics**).

Advice for Recommenders:
How to Write Great Letters of Recommendation

Whether you're a veteran LOR writer with hundreds of letters under your belt or writing one for the very first time, you'll find several useful tools in this section. We start with an overview of the legal issues surrounding letters of recommendation, evaluation and reference, which includes both a review of FERPA for academic LORs and a discussion of qualified privilege for employment references (**FAQ: Legal Issues**). Next, since so many individuals have been put in the frustrating position of writing "impossible" letters, we offer some advice that should eliminate 90% of those headaches (**FAQ: Managing Borderline/Unrecommendable Recommendees**). Finally, we address the difficulty that LOR-writers face when asked to evaluate applicants for programs or disciplines that are outside of their own expertise. We surveyed graduate and professional schools about the qualities and traits that they look for in candidates; the resulting lists may provide useful clues about the most relevant attributes to accentuate in any given LOR (**Checklists of Qualities Desired by Various Institutions and Professional Disciplines**).

Advice for Ghostwriters:
How to Draft Great Letters of Recommendation

When you approached your professor or supervisor for a LOR, you were hoping for a "Yes," although you were also prepared to hear "No." What you weren't expecting was the recommender's suggestion that you—the applicant—take a hand in drafting your own letter. If you are comfortable with this arrangement (and not everybody will be), read this chapter carefully. You'll find a rundown of typical missteps that inexperienced LOR-writers commit (**Common Mistakes and Omissions**)—including the microscopically subtle ways in which your use of language might be sabotaging the positive tone of your letter (**Avoiding LOR Language Pitfalls**). Finally, if you're completely at a loss as to how to start writing a LOR, we end with a couple of templates that will literally talk you, paragraph by paragraph, through the normal order of things for both academic and business recommendations (**Templates: Generic Letter of Recommendation**).

Sample Letters of Recommendation

In the second half of the book, you'll find 40+ sample letters of recommendation for situations ranging from high school scholarships to post-graduate employment and letters of commendation for business. You may choose to flip straight to the letters whose subject matter and intended audience are closest to your own (check out the subheadings at the top left corner of the page spreads). Alternately, you can browse the samples at random to get an idea of how LORs that share the basic structure can diverge widely in formality, tone, and emphasis.

HOW TO USE THIS BOOK

We surveyed a few hundred professors, asking them, "What was your worst-ever LOR experience?" The response was fantastic, so we've included the best of those stories—the ones most likely to inspire horrified laughter. Look for these anecdotes in the margins of the "Advice for Letter Seekers" chapter, and wherever you see this icon.

Sometimes, simply getting the answer to a Frequently Asked Question doesn't quite do it. When people don't like the answer, a hundred "what if..." and "but I heard somewhere that ..." objections instantly spring up. So we've assembled the most Frequently *Argued* Questions, with the aim of separating the true exceptions from the merely hopeful protests. Look for this FAQ icon in the margin—that's where we'll be doing our best to clarify the most common points of confusion that come up around LORs.

Terminology

Throughout the book, we occasionally abbreviate common phrases for the sake of brevity. LOR, of course, refers to letter of recommendation. GSI and TA stand in for graduate student instructor and teaching assistant, respectively. "Adcom" is a shortened form of admissions committee. "Referee" indicates the person who is asked to provide a work or academic reference. And FERPA, which we discuss extensively in the "Advice for Recommenders" section, is the acronym for the Family and Educational Privacy Act of 1974.

ABOUT THE AUTHORS

Don Osborne is the President and Founder of INQUARTA, a leading graduate school admissions advising service specializing in MBA, medical, allied health, law and other graduate programs. INQUARTA (www.inquarta. com) is the largest private graduate school advising service in the United States and has served more than 2,000 students seeking acceptance to top grad school programs. Drawing on over 20 years of advising experience, Don has developed the MBA Success system, a multidimensional approach to application strategy.

Don is a popular speaker on college campuses and has given hundreds of seminars on graduate and professional school admissions. He has twice been invited to be a workshop speaker at the International Golden Key convention of 1,200 club officers and members from all over the world.

Prior to founding INQUARTA, Don was a member of The Princeton Review faculty, the co-author of The Princeton Review MCAT Verbal course, author of the Verbal Accelerator program, and a Teacher Trainer for MCAT Verbal, LSAT, and GMAT.

Lilly Chow has over twelve years of editing experience, which includes managing content for both print journalism and Internet sites. She graduated from the University of California, Irvine, with both a bachelor's and Master's Degree in Comparative Literature. Subsequently, Lilly helped develop web content for Qian Yang International, a media/film production company.

Since 1999, when she began working as Managing Editor at IN-QUARTA's Irvine office, Lilly has assisted more than 300 clients to articulate and express their dreams of pursuing graduate and professional education. In 2002, she opened a satellite office of INQUARTA in Northern California, where she served as Director and Head Counselor.

ADVICE FOR LETTER SEEKERS:
How to Get Great Letters of Recommendation

The real question is: What helps me decide whether or not I will write a recommendation for a student? Here are some of the ways NOT to behave if students want a professor to agree to give them a recommendation in the first place. The "rules" I state below are all based on my personal experience, sadly enough. They are unusually egregious violations of common sense. Milder versions of these violations are much more common, and are generally enough to convince me that I'd rather not inflict the student on anyone else.

How Not to Impress A Professor

1. Fail a course that the professor teaches by ceasing to attend class or hand in any work after midterms, and then show up a week before finals (having missed the withdrawal deadline) and ask for an Incomplete with the excuse that you were "really busy this semester."
2. Show up an hour late for a midterm that lasts an hour and a half.
3. Send emails to the professor with the salutation "Yo" or "Hey there."
4. Copy a proposal from the Internet which the professor discovers you've plagiarized.
5. Use class time to catch up on your sleep.
6. Regularly show up late to class, fail to do the reading, and have no relevant answers when called on in class to participate in discussion.
7. Copy the problem set of another student in the class and hand it in as your own work.
8. Come to the professor and demand a higher grade because the class they teach is in the biological sciences, and biology classes are easy, so you deserve a higher grade, even if you failed to hand in the work.
9. Vociferously argue that the professor is wrong about something, even after he has patiently explained it to you for the third time, and shown you relevant references in textbooks that support his argument.
10. Show up two weeks after classes have begun, and explain that you didn't know when the semester started.

– Dr. Hillel Chiel
Case Western Reserve University

PREAMBLE: HOW TO DESERVE A
GREAT LETTER OF RECOMMENDATION

Some people choose to think of the LOR as a chore. They end up finding a thousand and one reasons to procrastinate, making the process far more burdensome than it has to be.

What's the alternative? Well, what if you saw the LOR as an opportunity to become comfortable with the professional you'd like to become?

Asking for a letter of recommendation is a time-honored ritual that introduces students to the reality that their future success will hinge on interdependent interaction. In fact, one could even say that the LOR will do more to prepare students for their careers than anything else in the application process.

Some people might dispute this, pointing out that plenty of professional skills are required to put together a polished personal statement, resume, or shortlist of schools. Now, we would never argue against the importance of writing a tightly focused statement of purpose—or that the application and resume should be proofread and revised until they are impeccable. We agree that it requires a certain level of maturity and focus to conduct the due diligence and cost-benefit analysis necessary to research and evaluate suitable graduate programs. We believe that interview prep is essential.[1] All of these correlate to truly valuable workplace skills. But the LOR—by definition—requires the cooperation of another individual. What we're talking about with the LOR is your first experience with the kind of reciprocal relationships that you'll need to advance in your career.

In other words, if you haven't yet mastered the art of give and take (especially the give part), the lesson starts here. Everything you've done is preparation for what you're about to do next. When your professor or work supervisor agrees to write you a letter of recommenda-

---

1. For more information on admissions advising, call 800-987-3279 x. 211 or visit www. inquarta.com.

tion, he or she is doing you a favor. They're providing you something of substantial value. In return for writing the letter, your recommenders really only want two things from you: 1) evidence of preparation and 2) follow-up. In other words, they appreciate a little consideration, appropriate expressions of gratitude, and the opportunity to get some closure on your situation. As favors go, this one is easy to pay back.

There really is a right way—and a wrong way—to ask for letters of recommendation. Nobody expects you to be perfect at it your first time out. But letter-writers do expect common courtesy. That includes empathy (do unto others as you would have them do unto you) and respect (deference, appreciation, actually listening to what they say—even when you don't like what they're saying).

Look, there's no shortage of advice out there about how to ask for a letter of recommendation. Even the most cursory Google search will bring up tons of career center handouts with titles like "Everything You Ever Wanted to Know about Letters of Recommendation." The information is readily available—but still, every year, students manage to irritate, alienate and offend the very letter writers whose support they're depending on. Why?

It's possible that they're going into the process blind and uninformed. More likely, they're approaching the recommender with the wrong attitude.

We believe that the single most important thing you can do in the LOR process is to set your intention to PROFESSIONALISM.

The tangible results? A happier recommender, who is much more likely to finish your LOR on time. It'll probably be a better letter, too.

As for intangible benefits, how about this one: *You don't have to be afraid about interacting with your superiors anymore.* In fact, once you understand the rules of the world you're aiming to enter, you'll laugh to think that procrastinating ever seemed like a good idea. Nothing builds confidence like the memory of success, and nothing's more appealing than confidence. So the next time you put yourself out there for consideration, whether it be for a scholarship, a grant, a great job offer, or a promotion, you're ten times more likely to succeed. Everything you've done is preparation for what you're about to do next.

Read through the table on the next page. The left column lists the standards of professional behavior that you can look forward to adopting as you proceed in your academic life and/or career. The right column shows you how you can start applying them as you embark on the process of seeking letters of recommendations. These statements embody the attitude of professionalism that successful applicants bring to the table in everything that they do.

PROFESSIONALISM: A QUICK RUNDOWN

- I present myself as capable, competent and trustworthy, and then live up to those expectations. I have earned a reputation for consistency and reliability because I am disciplined enough to stay on task until the job is done.

- I can evaluate a situation objectively—no matter what the implications are for my role and responsibilities.

- I educate myself thoroughly about the job/task in advance, so that I can avoid making inappropriate assumptions about what other people want or need.

- I am willing to demonstrate appropriate persistence. I operate in a transparent fashion by being very upfront about what I need to perform my role, and taking responsibility for keeping others updated on my progress.

- I respect the established hierarchies, and am eager to learn from those who have more knowledge or experience than I do. Ultimately, however, the approval I seek is my own, because my standards are higher than anybody else's.

- I take pride in the fact that the more effort I put in, the less effort others have to exert—however, I also know how to set appropriate boundaries. I refuse to be a pushover or doormat.

- I am ready to make the best of a bad situation. I resist the temptation to hide, shirk responsibility, or make excuses when something goes wrong. I acknowledge the power I have in any situation to control my emotions.

- I go above and beyond the call of duty to make life easier for others. Why? Because I can. I'm that good.

- I ask for the LOR without groveling or appearing presumptuous. I promise my recommenders that I will provide them with everything they'll need to write the letter in one sitting, and I deliver that prep package promptly.

- I am willing to ask, "Would you be able to write me a strong recommendation?" without being afraid of the answer. If my professor/supervisor tells me honestly that their letter would not benefit my application, I thank them and move on to Plan B.

- Because I know what common mistakes other letter-seekers make, I am far less likely to commit the same faux pas. For example, I know better than to buttonhole my recommenders at inopportune moments, give them less than a month to write the LOR, or list anybody as an academic or employment reference without preparing them first. I understand that the earlier I start strategizing LORs and building relationships, the more options I have.

- I resolve not to disappear mysteriously halfway through the process and suddenly reappear with no explanation. I know how to give my letter-writers direct reminders about my LOR deadlines.

- I am willing to try interacting with my supervisor/instructor, adult to adult, which means treating this LOR situation as a kind of friendly business transaction. I don't make demands. I don't plead. I don't make it too casual. I show that I appreciate my letter-writer's time. I know the difference between showing respect and being intimidated.

- I am willing to provide any information that the recommender says will help them write the LOR. If the recommender asks me to take a hand in drafting my own letter (i.e., ghostwriting) and that makes me uncomfortable, I decline that offer and start exploring other options.

- If for some reason a potential letter-writer is unable to fulfill his promise, I will not wallow in self-pity.

- I am willing to waive my right to read the letter because it will allow my letter-writer to write with complete candor. After all, I trust my recommender because I trust my own judgment in choosing him or her to evaluate me.

I get all sorts of contradictory information about how important letters of recommendation are.

That's because the importance of recommendations varies from school to school, and may even change over time. The bottom line: regardless of the LOR's actual influence on your admissions decision, the act of requesting and receiving a letter of recommendation is an exceedingly valuable exercise. This kind of respectful, thoughtful, mature interplay—speaking with candor and asking for it in return, making a genuine effort to anticipate other people's needs—is invaluable training for the next phase of your life, whatever it may be. In other words, even if admissions committees tossed these LORs away without ever reading them, you would have benefited from the process of requesting recommendations. It's never too early (or too late) to start practicing the art of professionalism.

By treating your recommenders with consideration and thoughtfulness, in a way that puts their convenience first, you build goodwill, and heaven knows you can't ever have too much of that. When your professor finally sits down to pound out your letter, the last thing you want is for any wisps of irritation to be clouding his brow because you only gave him a week to write the letter or because you forgot to tell him which scholarship you're applying for. After all, it's simply common sense: if you want these letters to describe you as a smart and mature individual, don't provide your recommenders with any evidence to the contrary during this process.

What does it take to get an outstanding LOR from a prof? How can I "wow" a prof besides going to office hours?

Let's dispel this myth right now. You can't compel a good letter where one doesn't exist. You can't make up for a semester of passivity with one good meeting. Don't flatter yourself into believing that professors can't tell when you're being greasily insincere. You can't fool anybody into writing you a better LOR than you deserve.

I've been told that when I approach my prof about a recommendation, I should ask her: "Will you be able to write me a strong letter?" And if she says no, then I should withdraw my request. Just the idea makes me squirm.

In other words, you don't want to risk having a completely honest conversation. That's a valuable piece of information about yourself. (We're not kidding.) Congratulations! You've just identified a muscle that's crying out to be exercised.

Correct me if I'm wrong, but the prospect of asking this question makes you anxious because you're not 100% sure that the prof's answer will be yes. The possibility of being judged and found lacking is unbearable. Wouldn't it make sense, then, that you can make the situation bearable by taking the suspense out of it?

The key is to take control. If you are willing to train this

One of the worst examples was a student who asked me to write "one" LOR, and he ended up giving me more than ten forms to fill out for different graduate schools—and then did not give me particular instructions about which LORs I was supposed to send directly to schools, and which LORs I was supposed to hand over to him. I had to write the student multiple times to know what I was supposed to do, and I almost ended up telling him that I changed my mind and that it was too much of a burden to write these.
– Dr. Guillaume Chanfreau
UCLA

muscle, we're willing to show you how. It may feel a little funny the first time you do it, but it gets easier. The next section will show you three ways to be proactive.

CONVERSATIONAL SCRIPTS FOR REQUESTING LETTERS

A. I just started taking a class with a prof who I might want to ask for a LOR. But it's a huge lecture class.

Many students in large classes fake themselves out before the game even starts. They shy away from approaching the professor, assuming that all 500 of their classmates must be swamping him during office hours. Think again. You might be surprised by how few students take advantage of the opportunity to meet directly with their professors.

If you have no idea how to ask for a letter from a professor whom you know only as the distant figure at the bottom of the lecture hall, let us help you solve that problem.

The best time to start is during the first week of class. Here's a conversational script you can use to get the ball rolling.

1. Schedule a meeting with the recommender. A sample email appears below:

> Dear Professor Jones:
>
> I would like to schedule a brief 10-minute meeting with you regarding my plans for graduate school. Would you be available sometime in the next few days? Let me know what is convenient for you and I will confirm back right away! Thank you.
>
> Sincerely,
> Your name

To increase your chances of making a good impression on your potential recommender, make sure you show up for the meeting early. Start by asking him or her: "Is now a good time to talk?"

2. Have the following conversation:

> "Hello, Professor Jones. My name is John Sample. I'm currently taking your class, [name the course]. I'm a third-year Economics major, and I'm planning to apply to business school next year. I would very much like to include a letter of recommendation from you in my application. However, I do not feel comfortable asking you for a letter right now because we don't know each other very well.

I remember a perfectly bland letter to which the writer had attached a post-it that simply said "NO!"
– Dr. Michael Eisen
Lawrence Berkeley National Laboratory

"I would like to set up two 15-minute conversations during this quarter to talk about both my academic progress in your class, as well as my interests in business and my involvement in XYZ [community, volunteer, research, etc]. At the end of the quarter, if you feel comfortable, may I come back to ask you for a letter of recommendation at that time?"

3. Follow through.

If he or she agrees to this arrangement—and it's a rare professor who will turn down a polite request from a motivated student—do not fail to follow up on your proposed appointments. Confirm the time and date, show up punctually, and thank the professor for their time. If possible, draw connections between their research and your own professional interests, and let the conversation bloom. Ask them for their advice on graduate school. If you establish a friendly rapport with this recommender, he or she may even be open to continuing the conversation during another meeting or two. Take advantage of this! The more they know about you, the more persuasively they can recommend you to graduate programs.

B. The course was two semesters ago, and I never made a face-to-face connection with the professor.

Don't despair. It's not too late to build a relationship that can serve as a basis for a letter of recommendation. Substitute this for the first paragraph of the script above:

"Hello, Professor Jones. My name is John Sample, and I took your course, _____, in Winter Semester of last year. I am planning to apply to _____ in 200x. I had hoped to ask you for a letter of recommendation. However, I don't feel comfortable asking you for a letter because we don't know each other very well.

"I would like to set up two 15-minute conversations during this quarter..."

C. I'm taking a class with a prof who's really well-known in the field. A letter from her would probably look great on my app, but she's really intimidating ... and anyways, I'm still a year or more away from applying.

You live in the best of all possible worlds. Let your professors know that you would like to ask them for a LOR in a year's time. Then, in the spirit of genuine curiosity, ask them the following:

"If you were me, what would you do to earn a fabulous letter from a professor like you?"

"What should I do over the next twelve months to earn a fabulous letter from you?"

Your professors may be taken aback by this question. They may laugh it off by tossing off some general advice: "Oh, just work hard in my class. Get an A. Be sure to participate."

They may be testing you by giving you a vague response. Show them you're serious by asking them for specifics. Or, if that seems too presumptuous, you may want to shift the conversation into a third-person stance; ask your professors what previous students did to deserve such winning recommendations.

"Can you tell me about some of your past students—the ones you wrote the best letters for? What types of activities did they do? How well did you get to know them?"

Then listen carefully. Responses that are adjective-based ("Oh, that student was brilliant" or "He had a very innovative mind") are not as useful as responses filled with the nouns and verbs of activity ("She ended up taking three classes with me" "Even after she graduated, she continued to email me articles about new media, and actually introduced me to a few blogs I didn't know about before." or "His senior thesis was so impressive that I was happy to nominate him for the Chancellor's Undergraduate Award.") You want to follow in these stellar students' footsteps, and it's a lot easier to emulate actions than qualities.

It's very likely that the prof will mention long-term interaction as a common theme of his most memorable students. When he or she does, that's your cue to inquire about the possibility of working with the professor on a research project.

Tell the professor that you'd like to be one of those students. If the professor believes you're sincere, he or she will be intrigued enough to challenge you to try. Professors don't see this degree of initiative from students very often. Imagine how pleased they would be to describe your gumption in the letter of recommendation. More importantly, imagine the kind of guidance and mentoring you'd benefit from if you actually built the kind of relationship with this professor that we're describing. A great letter of recommendation is really just a "symptom" of a great relationship.

Of course, then your challenge is to follow through. If you declare that you're going to aim for the top and then … disappear, or fade out after a few setbacks, that's not going to look very good. If you're going to put the spotlight on yourself, be ready to perform.

You can't possibly be advising me to volunteer to do independent study projects with every one of my professors.

Of course not. That's clearly impossible—who has the time? Our point is that because you have a finite amount of "academic

 My biggest annoyance comes from students who took my class as freshmen along with 500 other people, and with whom I never had a face-to-face conversation. They suddenly appear as seniors asking for a letter. After all, what can I really say on their behalf—especially if it turns out that they got a B in the class? That I have no idea who they are except that 350 students did worse than they did in an introductory class?
– Dr. Stuart Dryer
University of Houston

I've seen some bizarre recommender choices, some which really called the applicant's judgment into question. One student sent us an LOR that had been written by his dentist. "Having been a friend of the family for many years, I can assure you that this student is a good citizen—a pillar of the community. Also, he has terrific dental hygiene."
– Dr. Gregory Weiss
UC Irvine

capital" to spend, it's your responsibility to invest it wisely. In fact, you should plan it out beforehand. A year or two before you decide to apply to grad programs is the time to be asking yourself: "Whose recommendation would serve my application the best?" You narrow the field to a couple of professors who have a personality that would motivate you to do good work, and you gauge the relevance of their research against your own academic interests and future plans. You target the most likely suspects, and then you go after them.

These are really high standards. Like, unrealistically high.

You can't win big by betting small. And if you are applying to a top-tier program, you practically need to be ranked in the top 1% by your recommender. Like we said, the best letters of recommendation are not written for students who have only taken one class with the faculty member. While it's possible to seriously impress a professor over the course of a single semester, especially in a smaller class, there's also a limit to how often you can show up to office hours without coming across as brown-nosing (or not paying attention in lecture).

When professors write sentences such as "Jane Student is one of the top 10 students I have worked with in my career," you can bet that they're not thinking about how Jane beat the curve on that killer multiple-choice final exam or even how she raised her hand to speak at every opportunity. Aceing tests and thoughtful, enthusiastic participation are a good start, but they're not "Best in Show" good. That kind of performance will get you a hearty "above average," maybe even an "excellent"—but never "outstanding" or "extraordinary."

The larger the class, therefore, the more seriously you should consider approaching the professor directly to ask this important question: "What else can I do to make myself memorable academically in your eyes?"

FAQ: CHOOSING RECOMMENDERS

I'm going to ask my GSI / TA to write my letter of recommendation, since she knows me much better than the professor.

Hmm … are you sure you want to do that?

Why—is that a bad idea?

Well, it's true that a GSI can write a much more informed letter, because she's the one who graded all your papers and exams, and saw how much you participated during discussion section. But grad schools prefer to get LORs from full professors. Because they've had a longer teaching career, professors can rate your academic potential more objectively than a teaching assistant who may have only taught a few classes.

But the professor who taught the class doesn't know me from

Adam! I never went to his office hours because I was trying to get to know the GSI instead!

Relax—all's not lost. Ask your GSI if it would be possible to get the professor to co-sign the letter. She's probably very familiar with this practice, in which she drafts all or part of the letter using the pronoun "we" and then forwards it to the professor for his final comments and signature. This way, you can get a letter that contains the detailed insights of the teaching assistant—along with the endorsement of the professor.

When you suggest the co-signing option to your GSI, offer to do the footwork of approaching the professor and giving him your LOR prep package as well.

Maybe I can just email him about this new situation, and give the LOR prep package to the department secretary to put in his mailbox.

Why are you trying to avoid him? Are you afraid the meeting will be awkward and chilly, and he'll say, "I really don't know who you are."

Something like that.

Look, do your best to set up a face-to-face meeting, regardless. After all, the professor is putting his name on the letter. Give him at least one opportunity to look you in the eye and get a feel for your personality. If anything, since the GSI has already done the work of getting to know you, it should lighten the pressure for both of you in that meeting; the prof doesn't have to interview you intensively about your motivations for pursuing graduate study and you don't have to try to condense your life story into a few minutes.

Remember, a co-signed letter is not your secret weapon for avoiding the professor altogether. It should be, instead, a collaboration between three people instead of two. As the person making the request, it's your responsibility to make the GSI and professor feel as comfortable as possible about doing you this favor.

I keep hearing that VIP letters aren't a good idea. But the doctor that I shadowed last year was recently appointed to the President's Council on Bioethics—and it's not like he doesn't remember me. He may not know me as well as the Physician Assistant at the clinic where I volunteered, but he told me repeatedly that he thinks I'll make a great doctor.

Take a look at the discipline-specific checklists (starting on p. 63). They list the qualities and character traits that the admissions committee wants to know that you possess. Ask yourself honestly whether the M.D. or the PA has more firsthand knowledge of your ability to function in a health care environment, as well as how those skills have developed over time. The ideal recommender is usually the

A post-doc in the lab of a colleague of mine was looking for a job. She had listed me as a referee, but had not told me of this. I received a request for a LOR, and naturally went straight to my colleague to ask if he knew his post-doc was looking for another job. He was aware of the situation, and in-fact had recommended that she list me as a referee. I explained to him that I didn't mind being a referee, but at the very least she should have asked me, and sent me a copy of her CV, so I have something to write about in a LOR. A few days later she requested to meet with me personally to apologize, and I did end up writing a LOR. However, the tone of my letter was not as positive as it could have been, if she had communicated with everyone in the first place.
– Anonymous

person who's spent the most time directly supervising your work or evaluating your performance.

But that physician's an alum of the University of X, which is my top choice school.

Contrary to popular belief, letters from alumni don't necessarily carry more influence than other recommendations. On this issue, admissions committees are pretty unanimous: they prefer to read letters from people who have in-depth knowledge of your character and potential.

Even if he just donated $5 million to the university and they're planning to name the new student union after him?

If this person truly needs no introduction, go ahead and get a letter from him; have him send it separately to the relevant med school. If this alumnus really does have the kind of pull at his alma mater that you believe he does, his recommendation surely can't hurt. The deeper his influence at one school, however, the less effective it will be anywhere else. For all your other applications, the PA's recommendation would be the better choice to round out your LOR dossier.

I made a great connection with this visiting lecturer, and he's promised to write me a glowing letter of recommendation! But I've heard that letters from part-time faculty won't help my application.

Your strategy around this letter depends heavily on what you're planning to use it for. Let's say you're looking for a LOR to help you get a job. Great! No problem! For most people outside of academia, seeing that your letter-writer has a Ph.D. is enough to assure them that this professor was well-qualified to rate your academic performance.

However, if you are planning to continue your education, you need to know that letters from adjunct/part-time faculty tend to hold less value in the admissions decision-making process. This may not matter greatly for applicants to professional schools. However, if you're applying to graduate programs, where you are expected to produce letters from well-regarded, tenured professors in your field, a LOR from a "mere" lecturer would raise a few eyebrows. It would suggest that you apparently did not seek out mentoring from a full professor—and the logical follow-up question would be: Well, why not? Graduate admissions committees know very well who their peers are, and a recommender's position in the academy does matter, for several reasons.

The worst was from a writer who said, "This is the worst student who has ever worked with me. In one year she accomplished absolutely nothing. I know of no reason why you would want to admit her." Needless to say the applicant hadn't asked if her advisor could write her a GOOD letter as opposed to just a letter.
– Dr. Eric Hudson
MIT

I don't understand why a LOR from a part-time faculty member would be treated differently than a letter from a full-time professor.

Well, adjunct faculty tend to be at the beginning of their teaching career, which puts them at a disadvantage vis-à-vis tenured faculty in that they've simply worked with fewer students. The title of part-time/adjunct faculty is often given to graduate students who are responsible for lectures and running the course; this is very common in summer session classes. But it's not so much a matter of how many students a professor teaches, since adjunct faculty often get saddled with multiple core classes. What really matters is that part-time faculty tend to have less experience working one-on-one with students, in some cases because limitations are placed on their ability to supervise independent study projects. It's a fact: students are strongly encouraged to seek advising and career planning from full-time faculty members rather than part-time instructors. Lastly, visiting lecturers who commute from job to job also lack a "stable" student base against which to compare an applicant's performance.

Because colleges are increasingly relying on part-time faculty to teach their core classes, however, it's possible that some students might reach their junior year before they take a course in their major with a full tenured professor. For students with ambitions to pursue graduate studies, this state of affairs puts them at a distinct disadvantage. The solution is to be fiercely pro-active about making connections with full-time faculty members as a freshman or sophomore.

Note: The disadvantage presented by an adjunct faculty LOR can sometimes be mitigated if this professor is in the same field that you are aspiring to. Just because an adjunct faculty member doesn't have a permanent position doesn't mean that they do not have a reputation in the field. Especially at research institutions, even the adjunct faculty will have published articles or presented papers at conferences.

A student whom I had caught cheating asked me to write him a letter of recommendation. I told him that I might not be his best reference and suggested that he ask someone who didn't know him as a "cheater" to write the letter. He just looked at me and asked, "You'd put that in a letter?" Ah, yeah. I thought that if he's that dumb, I ought to write the letter, but I didn't.
— Dr. Vinita Dew
Truman State University

I have an embarrassment of riches—more willing recommenders than is required! The grad programs I'm applying to ask for a bare minimum of three letters, but they also say they'll accept a few additional recommendations. The more I send, the better, right? I'd hate to waste a good recommendation.

First of all, ask yourself (and your recommenders) whether the content of their letters would differ substantially enough to warrant sending out both. If you are beloved by several professors, you are a lucky student indeed. However, if they all love you in the same exact way, sending their too-similar letters would be redundant, and actually rob you of the chance to showcase alternate skill sets or personality traits from the perspective of other recommenders.

You may also want to deploy any "extra" letters in a more

strategic way. For example, if your application is placed on a waitlist, it could be very valuable to have a strong letter of recommendation in reserve. At that point in the process, the admissions committee is actively interested in getting additional material to help them sift out the stronger candidates on the waitlist; an additional statement from faculty testifying on your behalf could help make the difference.

I was tutoring a student privately, who was attempting to qualify for licensure in a medical subspecialty involving patient treatment. There is a substantial risk (and incidence!) of serious patient injury due to practitioners' errors in this specialty. We were working on a series of "exercises" the student had been given... when it slipped out that this was actually a take-home exam. I was shocked and immediately refused to continue with it. When time came to pay me for hours I had put in, there was a delay of several weeks, followed by a check that bounced! I wrote a stiff letter demanding a money order, which I got. End of story... until the student phoned me again months later and asked me to write a letter of recommendation for further study! What mental process could possibly be behind this I cannot imagine.
– Anonymous

I still keep in touch with my English teacher from my senior year of high school. She could write a great letter talking about my growth over the years.

A letter from a pastor or community member who has seen you grow up—that might work as a supplementary (i.e., non-academic) character reference to round out your portfolio of LORs. But a letter from a high school teacher would raise questions for most graduate and professional schools' admissions committees. They are operating on the assumption that anything that you were able to accomplish in high school you should be able to duplicate in college. It's no good to have been brilliant in Algebra II/Trig back in the day if you ended up flunking Statistics last semester. And even your touching loyalty in corresponding with old mentors could be seen as a red flag, as in: "Shouldn't the applicant be putting his time and energy to better use by developing relationships with his college professors?"

There is one exception to this rule: recommendations from high school instructors can often be acceptable if you are applying for prestigious, nationally competitive fellowships (e.g., Rhodes, Marshall). Such fellowship applications, which require up to eight letters, practically demands that the applicant think very strategically in terms of designating a specific "core theme" for each letter based on the particular recommender who can speak most eloquently about them. In that case, the high school teacher would be called upon to discuss the applicant's long-term growth OR the applicant's talents in an area that he may not have had the chance to pursue much in college (e.g., sports, debate club, drama).

The grad program I'm applying to requires two recommendations from faculty at my current university. But I've been out of school for a year and I'd rather submit two letters from professionals in my field. Both are amazing mentors who have really influenced me to go back to school. There's no question that they would be able to write better letters for me than any of my undergraduate professors—and that's what counts, right? The quality of the letters?

Yes, the quality of one's recommendations is extremely important. But so is the ability to follow instructions.

Think about it: Adcoms need to know how you perform in an academic context, because grad school is not merely a continuation of college. (If x represents the academic intensity and amount of reading that you had to do as an undergrad, think of grad school as x^3. When they talk about "academic rigor," they aren't kidding.) The admissions committee that you're trying to impress is made up of faculty members in your future department. You will be taking seminars with these professors; one of them is probably your future advisor. They want to hear about you from colleagues in their field—colleagues whose work with grad students on a daily basis (e.g., supervising advanced research, evaluating teaching, reading dissertations) qualifies them to evaluate your potential to perform at the same level.

If you have any interest in a getting a letter of acceptance, you'll submit one letter from one of your non-academic mentors (or maybe a single letter co-written by both?) only as a supplementary letter. Your two main letters must be from faculty members. That might mean that you have to go back and re-establish relationships with former professors (see "Conversational Scripts for Requesting Letters," p. 20). Depending on your situation, your best option might be to start fresh by enrolling in two post-baccalaureate/extension classes in your chosen field and schmoozing the hell out of those professors. If that seems like a lot of hoops to jump through to get into grad school, it's nothing compared to the hoops you'll be asked to jump through to get your master's or doctorate.

The person who knows me best was from my previous job, and that was three years ago. But if I have a letter that was written three years ago, that's too old.

Not necessarily. For some people, an effective LOR strategy may involve including an older letter to demonstrate that they have a history of good performance.

However, it's true that many academic admissions committees request LORs that were written no more than three years ago. (Can you really blame them? The more recent the letter, the more likely it is that the praise contained in it is fresh and relevant.) If you find yourself with a letter that's past the expiration date, the solution is simple: update your file by having your recommender rewrite that old letter. At the very least, you should ask him or her to change the date; the savvy applicants, however, will parlay this into an opportunity to sit down for a chat with their old recommenders to tell them the latest and greatest. The result? A letter whose updated content suggests a warm, long-standing relationship with mentors. That's the sign of an applicant who's already a consummate professional.

The MBA application specifies that I need a LOR from my current employer, but I just started this job two months ago. Not only would my new boss have very little to say about me, I'm also not sure I want the company to know that I might be leaving in a year.

Potential employers may not specify such stringent requirements, but hiring committees—quite reasonably—tend to find current information about an applicant's work performance more relevant than older evaluations. Like we said earlier, it's possible to use an older letter effectively to show consistency over the years, but be warned: if old letters is all you have, that's a red flag for hiring employers. They'll assume that you either haven't done anything recommendation-worthy in your current position, or that you have a terrible relationship with your supervisors.

If you're in a position where asking for a recommendation could jeopardize your relationship with your current boss, you should be able to make that clear to the potential employer or graduate school that you're applying to. Most of them will understand the delicacy of your situation and are willing to make exceptions, provided that you can offer another LOR of recent vintage.

A colleague who sometimes supervises my work has offered to write me a highly descriptive and very flattering letter. Our distinguished CEO, on the other hand, probably couldn't give me anything more than a perfunctory (though positive) letter. In other words, I have to choose either a great letter from a "nobody" or a halfway decent letter from a VIP. I'm really not sure which LOR would serve me better.

If you know for certain that recommendations don't count for much where you're applying, feel free to submit either letter. Otherwise, you're nearly always better off with a LOR from the person whom you have built a real relationship with. Remember: a relationship has to mean more than the fact that your letter-writer has warm and fuzzy feelings towards you. If you're applying for a position that is prestigious and competitive, you increase your chances of acceptance by presenting detailed recommendations from individuals who regularly guide and evaluate your work. The more people they have supervised in your position, the higher their credibility.

———————————

I just sent out all my applications! Now I can relax. It's such a relief to not have to treat every new professor like a potential recommender!

Are you sure you won't need an extra letter for waitlists? Cultivate those relationships anyway. It's not like attending office hours is a waste of your time if you want to get ahead in your classes. Remember what happened the last time you went to office hours? Your ulte-

The worst experience relates to a postdoctoral fellow I have. She had an otherwise strong letter of recommendation from her graduate advisor with the exception of a comment from the advisor that if this student hadn't spent so much time talking in the lab, rather than working, she would have had a more substantial thesis. I overlooked this at the time. But now, with NIH funding extremely tight, the postdoctoral fellow has been unsuccessful at obtaining fellowship grant support. Right now I am wondering why and I suspect that this single comment from her advisor in the letter of recommendation will haunt her for the rest of her career. The worse bit about this is that the postdoctorate fellow will never even know the reason why.
– Anonymous

rior motive, let's admit it, was to butter up the professor for a letter of recommendation. But during that visit, you asked about that point in lecture that went by too fast for you—and the prof clarified it for you. Or she looked over your outline, warned you that your thesis was too ambitious, and gave you a few ideas about how to streamline your argument. Maybe you even got a hint about what the final exam would focus on. It helped, didn't it?

Med schools say they want 1-2 letters from science faculty, but I'm not exactly sure if my Computer Science or Nutrition or Public Health professors would count as science faculty.

Check the "Coursework: Course Classification" section of the latest AMCAS Instruction Manual as a starting point to clarify your situation (Do a search for "AMCAS instruction manual" at http://www.aamc.org).

As you know, BCPM stands for Biology, Chemistry, Physics, and Mathematics; only classes in these academic departments can be used in calculating your science GPA on your medical school application. If the class in question falls under a BCPM grouping (e.g., Ecology is a subcategory of Biology, Astronomy is a subcategory of Physics), then a LOR from the professor who taught the class definitely counts as a science faculty letter.

On the other hand, professors who teach classes in Behavioral & Social Sciences are almost never considered science faculty.

And then there's wiggle room. If the class is categorized under Health Sciences, Natural/Physical Sciences, or Engineering, your bid to claim that professor as science faculty will depend heavily on: 1) whether the professor in question is trained as a scientist (i.e., biologist, chemist, physicist); 2) how much of the grade in that class was based on BCPM methodology; 3) how extensively the professor can comment on your classroom ability as a science learner.

If a med school feels that the LORs you've submitted do not satisfy their requirements, they will ask you to submit the recommendation(s) that they believe to be missing. If your situation is ambiguous, check with individual schools about their requirements early on, so that you can avoid the scenario of scrambling for LORs late in the game.

FAQ: BUREAUCRATIC ISSUES

My pre-health advising office will take care of it for me.

Are you sure? Pre-health programs at colleges and universities differ widely in how they handle LORs for pre-meds. Some schools

It is well known that foreign students often change schools to try to "move up" a few notches in the school rankings. I had a grad student working in my lab for half a year, when he decided to apply to another school. Not only did he propose to break the research agreement we had, he asked me for a letter of recommendation! I told him I would be at best ambivalent, but I wrote him a letter. He got accepted to that school. Then six months after he got there, I got an email from him that he was applying to yet another school, one slight step higher on the ladder, and he wanted yet another letter of recommendation from me! Here is a general piece of advice: if you are burning your bridges, don't ask the people you are burning to write you a letter.
– Dr. David Snoke
University of Pittsburgh

One of the saddest cases for me was a student who had taken a class from me one summer term; the class was for entering honors freshmen who wanted to get an early start on their college career. He came to me years later as a senior, asking for a recommendation. I hadn't seen him in the intervening years, and I told him that a letter based on a summer class so many years ago wouldn't carry much weight. Then it came out that during his entire time in college, he thought I was the only professor who even knew his name.
— Dr. Steven Goates
Brigham Young University

simply lack any advising resources whatsoever, which means that your only campus recourse for organizational assistance with your LORs may be the Career Center. At the other extreme, some pre-professional health careers offices are so hands-on that they require you to interview with them before you can get approval to get any letters from instructors of pre-med courses. (By culling the number of pre-meds they offer support to, they can goose up their pre-med acceptance rates. Harsh but true.) Thankfully, most pre-med advising offices fall somewhere in between, but you still owe it to yourself to find out early on what their policies are. Many offices will help guarantee confidentiality by receiving, storing, and mailing your professor's LORs with the official seal—but some offices limit the number of recommendations they'll handle for each pre-med, while others mail out the entire file to every school you designate (which could be a problem if certain grad programs specify a maximum number of letters that they'll receive). The earlier you learn about any quirks that your university's pre-med office has, the sooner you can make arrangements to work around those quirks, if necessary.

I've heard that adcoms don't review the application until all LORs are received. Whew! That gives me a few extra weeks to work on my application.

Admissions committees understand that the postal service doesn't always cooperate with an applicant's intentions; most are willing to make allowances for a stray document. However, if several pieces of your application come in after the deadline, it's likely to reflect badly on you as a sign of disorganization.

Does it make a difference if my recommenders answer the online questions individually or send a centralized letter?

Most adcoms state that they do not have a preference about which format they receive LORs in—paper or online, multi-question or letter. As long as the recommender answers the specific questions listed on their LOR forms, they're satisfied.

Many professors, however, have told us that they find the new online applications to be very onerous and time-consuming. Recommenders who are feeling overwhelmed may be more likely to agree to your LOR request if you give them the option of writing the simpler "generic" letter that can be mailed or transmitted to several institutions at once.

HOW CAN I MAKE LIFE EASIER FOR MY RECOMMENDERS?

The more organized you are, the less time it will take to complete this section of your application. First, think deadlines. Although you won't need letters of recommendation until you apply, do keep in mind that one of the most common causes of a delay in the admissions process is a tardy recommender. For this reason, you must give your recommenders at least 30 days to write the letter. Take that extra time into account when you tell them the date that you need the letters. Plan to call your recommenders around the time of the deadline, or just a bit before, reminding them to complete their letters on time. A cheerful, tactful tone will go a long way.

Of course, you will need to give your recommenders much more than a deadline if you want them to write you the best possible letter. Try to supply them with all the necessary information that they would need to write your letter in one sitting. The easier you make the process for them, the more likely they are to finish the letter on time. It only takes a little extra time to organize the process for yourself and for your recommenders in advance, and it helps you avoid a lot of frustration later on.

For each recommender, prepare a package composed of the following materials:

1. A **reference release form** officially giving your recommender permission to discuss in the letter what he or she deems necessary. If your university doesn't have a standard form, take a look at the template we've included on p. 36 and adapt it for your own purposes.

2. Your **resume** describing your professional accomplishments, coursework, honors and degrees.

3. A copy of your **personal statement** (a typed rough draft is OK).

4. A work or academic **project, or other item specific to your relationship with the recommender**. The goal here is to refresh the recommender's memory about you by including something this person may have used in the past to evaluate you in some way.

5. A **summary of the Core Themes** of your application. Explain what makes you special or unusual as a candidate. Emphasize those items in your record that are most significant to the application and also those that you feel the recommender can

 The most common mistake students make is to not tell the professor what field they are applying to. I never check this until I sit to write the statement, and frankly, I am not about to stop and ask once I start.

Once, I even stated in the recommendation itself that I had no idea what program this particular student was applying for--as an example of this student not thinking about what he was doing.
– Anonymous

clarify or elaborate upon most effectively. (You're not exactly telling the recommender what to write; you're just sharing with them what you think would maximize your chances of gaining admission.)

6. **Letter of Recommendation form** downloaded from the program website, usually as part of the application. These forms contain a grid where the recommender will rank your abilities in areas ranging from academic potential to creativity and self-discipline. It will also include the waiver statement.

7. **Cover letter, and a stamped self-addressed envelope.** Once you have compiled these materials, write an individualized cover letter to each recommender. The letter should express thanks and explain the contents of the package. It should give the writer clear instructions on what to do with the completed letter.

For your reference, we have included a sample cover letter below, followed by a sample resume and an example of a Core Themes page. Do not use this cover letter verbatim; doing so will make you look lazy and unethical.

FAQ: ASSEMBLING THE LOR PREP PACKAGE

I'm all ready. I'm planning to give my recommender my statement of intent, transcript, a paper of mine that she graded—to remind her of my work, SASE envelopes, forms and instructions, waivers, a spreadsheet w/ deadlines, and a little gift.

Whoa, there. Hold off on the gift until after she's written the LOR. Giving little tokens of your appreciation as you request the letter—or at any point while they're still writing it—can be misconstrued. Recommenders generally understand that you don't mean the gift as a bribe. Still—best to avoid the appearance of impropriety. There's nothing improper, however, about a nicely handwritten card thanking them in advance for their letter—especially if you're looking for ways to remind your recommender the deadline is coming up.

By the way, if you're racking your brain about what to give recommenders as a gift, we hear that professors like to be thanked with candy. Or a gift card from the local coffeeshop.

I'm asking for job references from a prof and an employer. It's not for grad school, so my LOR prep package doesn't need to be so complicated, right?

As a general rule, the more info you give your recommender, the more targeted a letter they can write. After all, they can always disregard any materials that seem less relevant to them.

Professors who are asked to write for non-academic situations especially appreciate some background on the company or industry you're trying to crack. Include a brochure of the company, or even printouts of the company's mission statement or the job description from the website. You'd be surprised how many professors complain that their students forget to tell them what program or job they need a recommendation for!

My recommender offered to critique my statement of purpose; she gave me a bunch of suggestions and told me to show her the revisions. I don't want to hurt her feelings, but I think my statement is perfect right now. Her advice also conflicts with what other recommenders have told me. I really don't know how to handle this. I don't want this professor saying I'm uncooperative in her LOR.

You're right—you don't want to antagonize your recommender, especially when she's extended a very generous offer to help advise you on the content of your application. We suggest that you accept her critique graciously (and show her the revisions—if that's what she wants). And when we say you should make the revisions, we don't mean it as a cynical ploy to stay in your recommender's good graces. First of all, if this professor has served on admissions committees in the past, she could be providing you with some very important clues about what other adcoms will respond to in your statement.

In the end, the only person who knows which version of your statement you submit as part of your application is you. Nobody can force you to submit "their" version. But think of this exercise as a lesson in keeping a very open mind. Operate on the assumption that there's always room for improvement. Is it possible that the revised version is slightly better than what came before?

I gave my prof my LOR prep package with all the forms two months ago, and the letter hasn't shown up in my LOR service account yet. The letter's due in a week. I'm getting really nervous.

Tardy letters of recommendation are second only to missing transcripts when it comes to causing application delays. How do you make sure that this doesn't happen to you?

At the very least, make sure that your deadline is clearly marked (in several places) on the LOR prep packages that you give your recommenders. Now, if that simple act were enough to guarantee that all recommender would turn in their LOR on time, this

 We were reviewing an application from someone who listed an email address that was a bit too intimate. Something along the lines of "likestosweatatnight@ hotmail.com." (I've changed the address substantially, but the actual address referred to a particular smell!) We all felt a bit weirded out by it, and deferred consideration for another week.
— Anonymous

would be a lovely world indeed! The harsh reality is that the best recommenders tend to be the busiest people, and LORs can easily slip down their list of priorities. Sometimes, when life gets in the way, it even slips off their agenda completely. College professors are especially notorious for allowing LOR requests to get lost in their pile of administrative demands. That's why applicants who have the luxury of time should consider giving their recommenders an artificially early deadline. For example, if you're requesting the LOR in late May and the absolute deadline is August 31st, tell your letter-writer that you need it by the middle or end of July. That way, you'll give them a generous six to eight weeks, but also maintain a buffer zone for your own peace of mind. You may need that extra time to give your recommender one final chance to write the letter—or in the worst case scenario, to approach and prepare another recommender.

Now, if a recommender has agreed to write you a letter, you should not be afraid to remind them in a gentle way. Keep your eye on the deadline; as it approaches, give your recommender a heads up. You're not likely to insult anybody if you send a simple email, a week or so before the deadline, saying, "Hi, I just wanted to send a friendly reminder that my letter is due on [date]. Thanks again for agreeing to write a recommendation for me." Make sure you sign the email with your full name.

But I've already sent two emails!

If you don't get a response to an e-mail after several days, it may have fallen into the recommender's junk mail box. Try a phone call; ask him or her if there's anything else that you can provide them to make their letter-writing process easier.

I don't want to be a pain in the ass.

Final suggestion: If you have the opportunity to give your recommenders your LOR prep packages in person, you may want to ask them at that time how they'd like to be reminded about the deadline. They may be grateful for the opportunity to specify, for example, that they prefer phone calls to emails, or that the reminder should be timed to arrive after they turn in a big grant application or finish grading final exams. They may even tell you that a certain degree of persistence and assertiveness will be necessary. Some professors confided to us that they need to be "pestered to death" about LORs—because they have such a bad habit of procrastinating this task. (Just to be clear here: be sure to get a recommender's express permission before you indulge in any sort of nagging!)

One student sent me his resume and list of grad schools just before Thanksgiving. In his note he told me that he was supplying me with this information so that I could write his letter over the weekend (as if I had nothing better to do!) since his letters were due in a week. When I told him that I would need more time, his curt reply was "Do your best. Just remember that the letters are due on December 1st."
– Dr. Jeanne Perry
UCLA

TEMPLATE: COVER LETTER FOR LOR PREP PACKAGE

DO NOT USE VERBATIM

[date]

[recommender's address]

Dear [name of recommender]:

Thank you for supporting my application. Your letter will have a profound influence on the decision of the admissions committees. I appreciate very much the time you have spent helping me to realize my goal of [winning a scholarship/being accepted to a graduate program/getting hired at XYZ company/etc.].

This package contains several items, including: 1) the personal statement that is the core of my application; 2) a resume summing up my professional experience; 3) a page focusing on the core themes of my application, and areas of particular concentration; and 4) a copy of work I recently completed for you [mention any other materials you are including here].

I have made an effort to include these items in order to provide you with all the specific information you will need to write the letter. However, if there is anything else you think you will need, please let me know.

As you know, admissions committees find particularly helpful letters of recommendation that provide (1) a detailed description of our relationship, and 2) a comparison between me and other applicants pursuing similar graduate or professional goals. This comparison can be qualitative or quantitative, including comments about reasoning skills or about my academic performance relative to other applicants you have worked with.

The letter itself would ideally include comments tied to a specific project, assignment, or other work of mine that you have personally reviewed.

[Optional: If there is some issue you particularly need this recommender to discuss, identify it here and explain why it is important that this item be mentioned in the recommendation letter.]

I will be submitting my applications in [month], so I will need the letter of recommendation to be sent [describe mailing instructions in detail] no later than [date].

Again, should you have any questions whatsoever, or if you would like additional information, please contact me at [email address] or [phone number].

Sincerely,

[your signature]
Enclosures

PS: I will follow up with you on [date] by email to make sure that all is well.

DO NOT USE VERBATIM

TEMPLATE: REFERENCE RELEASE FORM

Reference Release Form

I request that Professor _____ serve as a reference for me. Professor _____ _____ has my permission to disclose any personally identifiable information related to my academic performance (including but not limited to grades, GPA, class rank) in a letter of reference or recommendation. I authorize release of this letter to:

____ all educational institutions

____ all prospective employers

____ other _____

_____   _____
Signature   Date

SAMPLE RESUME

JOHN SAMPLE

2222 Sidecreek Street * Knowlwood, TN 37235 # (615) 555-0650 * jsample07@vanderbilt.edu

OBJECTIVE

To attend a top-tier MBA program with an emphasis in Entrepreneurial Studies, and ultimately to establish my own business as a renewable energy consultant.

EDUCATION

VANDERBILT UNIVERSITY, NASHVILLE, TENNESSEE
B.A., **Economics and Environmental Engineering**. Degree expected June 2007
Cumulative GPA: 3.40

EXPERIENCE

Accounts Payable Analyst. ARGO HYDRAULICS, Knowlwood, TN. 2006–2007
- Receive and process all cash, check and credit card transactions and vendor invoices into database; reconcile and verify receipts on a weekly basis.
- Match goods received to the invoice, securing approval for payment as well as accurate and timely payment to the vendors.
- Prepare written reports and spreadsheets involving macros analyzing variance from Actual to Budgeted results on a monthly and YTD basis.
- Identify and track the causes of misapplied payments. My proposed streamlining of ledger oversight procedures successfully eliminated 30% of accounting discrepancies.

Philanthropy Chair. ALPHA GAMMA SIGMA – VANDERBILT CHAPTER, Nashville, TN. 2006
- Initiated a new program, "AGS Construction Saturdays," a monthly commitment to help on the local Habitat for Humanity construction sites.
- Expanded participation in fraternity's weekly tutoring program for at-risk middle school students from 15 to 40 regular volunteers.
- Coordinated annual food and clothing drives, increasing donations by 300% over previous record.

ACTIVITIES
- **Member**, Alpha Gamma Sigma National Fraternity (Fall 2003–present)
- **Member**, Vanderbilt Undergraduate Business Association (2005–2006)
- **Disc Jockey**, WRVU 91.1 FM (2005–present)
  - Produce, host and direct live radio music show, featuring local indie rock bands.
- Intramural baseball

COMPUTER LITERACY
- Microsoft Word, Power Point, QuickBooks Premier

SAMPLE CORE THEMES SUMMARY

John Sample Core Themes

Focused
- Future Goals
    - Determined to establish energy consultancy firm specializing in renewable and green technologies
    - Recognize the growth potential of energy efficiency and alternative fuel industries as well as "green citizenship" models
    - Envision offering resource assessment and development, project development and Management, utility integration, performance evaluation and systems analyses for corporate clients in Appalachia

Diverse Intellectual Curiosity
- Double major in Economics and Environmental Engineering
- Passionate about identifying and promoting the use of emerging technologies as good business sense

Superior Communication Skills
- Fine-tuned verbal and communication skills from experience as live radio announcer
- Interpersonal skills: Skilled at motivating diverse people to live up to their best intentions

Strong Quantitative Skills
- Two years of work experience as an Accounts Payable Analyst have immersed me in the practical application of General Accounting principles and procedures
- As Economics major, took two semesters of Calculus and Econometrics
- As Engineering major, took Probabilistic & Numerical Methods course

Demonstrated Leadership
- As philanthropy chair of Alpha Gamma Sigma Fraternity, assumed responsibility for organizing the community service involvement of 86 fellow students
- Successfully increased participation in all of the fraternity's traditional philanthropic activities (tutoring program, donation drives, charity 10K run)
- Proposed and executed a new program to support the local Habitat for Humanity affiliate; "AGS Construction Saturdays" was a two-month campaign that ultimately involved 30 fraternity brothers donating a total of 400 man-hours of labor.

FAQ: WAIVERS AND LOGISTICS

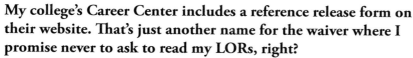

My college's Career Center includes a reference release form on their website. That's just another name for the waiver where I promise never to ask to read my LORs, right?

Actually, you're referring to two separate issues that are almost never addressed on a single document. The first form is to help safeguard your privacy. The second form is to give your LOR writer the freedom to write a completely candid letter—the kind which is most prized by admissions committees.

Here's the breakdown: Back in 1974, the U.S. Congress passed a piece of legislation known as the Family and Educational Privacy Act (FERPA) that guarantees students the right to inspect and review the educational records that their colleges are maintaining on them, as well as some control over who else gets to know the information contained there. Once you turned 18 (or started attending a postsecondary institution), FERPA gave you the key to the cabinet where your grades and GPA are stored. Technically, university employees are not allowed to divulge your educational record to anyone (not even to your parents). Which also means, technically, that in order for your professors to discuss your grade or GPA or academic performance with anybody else, they need your written authorization.

What do you mean by "educational record"?

By the strictest definition of FERPA, your educational record includes: the grades and GPAs on your transcript, your course schedule, your academic status, your Social Security and student ID numbers. But the list actually goes on and on.[2] Essentially, the only information that university employees are always allowed to divulge about you without your specific permission is your name, whether you're an undergrad or grad student, and when you started attending this school.

So even after your prof or TA has verbally agreed to write you a LOR, you should still officially request in writing that he or she serve as your reference; you can use that same document to authorize them to discuss "personally identifiable" information in your educational record.

It seems so ridiculous that I have to give my prof permission to talk about my class performance in a LOR.

You're right—it hasn't always been this way, and no doubt hundreds of recommendations are still probably written every day without these release forms. For better or for worse, however, this extra layer of formality is becoming an increasingly common part of

---

2. If you're interested in the types of data that *can* be considered protected by FERPA, take a look at p. 52. If you want to know specifically what your college or university has defined as protected information, ask your registrar.

the academic LOR process. If nothing else, by taking the initiative to provide your prof with legal cover, you can probably help take a little pressure off him or her. And anything you can do to smooth out the process for them will be appreciated.

My friend who goes to a different college says he can't find this release form anywhere.

If your school doesn't have a standard FERPA form that officially gives your recommender/reference permission to furnish info to a third party (i.e., admissions committees and/or potential employers), you can whip up your own very easily.[3] Take a look at the sample form on p. 36. It doesn't need to get very fancy. As you can see, our sample letter includes all four essential elements of a FERPA release form, namely: 1) the type of information that can be released, 2) for what purpose, 3) to whom, and 4) your signature with date.

Unless you have genuine fears about your academic information falling into the wrong hands, it's a good idea to authorize broadly, so that you don't have to keep coming back to this particular professor with additional FERPA release forms when you need letters for scholarships, grant proposals, employment references, etc.

So that's the release form. You're saying this is different from the LOR confidentiality form.

Yep. Here's the deal. Once the LOR is written, it also becomes part of your educational record. If you want to know why, it's because the letter contains information directly related to a student (you) about the student's tenure at the University, because it's written by those acting for the college or university (your recommender), and because it's maintained by that educational agency or institution. And since the LOR is part of your educational record, it becomes another item that FERPA technically gives you the right to inspect.

So you're saying I *do* have the right to read my LORs.

Yes, unless you decide to sign away that right in advance. And here's the rub: many professors feel more comfortable writing letters for applicants if they know that the recommendee will never read it. They prefer that it be a confidential correspondence between them and the intended recipient. This is where the waiver comes in (a.k.a. the Optional Waiver of Right of Access). When you sign the waiver, you're giving up your FERPA right to inspect or review that LOR.

I don't get it. What are professors afraid that I'd do with the letter if I read it?

Some students believe that professors demand that you waive access to their LORs because they're wary about being confronted if you don't like what they say about you.

---

3. The form is usually known as the Student Reference/LOR Request or the FERPA Release; ask the Career Center or your departmental advisor.

More likely, though, it's that professors are concerned about their hard work going to waste. Applicants who want to improve their chances wouldn't keep a reference letter in their file if they knew that it wasn't entirely complimentary, right? If all students inspected every letter that was written for them, many LORs would get tossed—and then, from the professor's point of view, what was the point of writing the letter in the first place?

Here's an analogy: How would you feel about writing an on-line product review if you knew that the webmaster was likely to delete any write-up that was even vaguely negative? If you thought there was a chance that nobody would ever get to read your review, you might think twice about volunteering to write it in the first place; at the very least, you'd be hesitant about offering a truly honest opinion. By the same logic, professors prefer that students waive their right to read LORs because they don't want their letters to be kidnapped on the way to their destination. So to speak.

So what does a professor do when asked to pen a letter for a student whom he cannot support wholeheartedly—if he thinks there's the slightest chance that the student will read it? He protects himself. Over the years, LOR writers have learned to avoid disparaging applicants outright, and LOR recipients have learned to adjust their "reading glasses" to read between the lines. I'm talking here about the Intentionally Ambiguous Phrase that says two things at once. A quick skim (or a naïve reader) will perceive nothing but praise; upon deeper examination, the truth materializes slyly. Here's a favorite example: "You'll be very lucky if you can get this person to work for you."

Get it?

It's an extremely subtle art. Profs take unseemly delight in these exquisitely-turned phrases, these lovingly camouflaged red flags. They collect them, chuckle over them at faculty meetings, and email them to each other like chain letters.[4] And they do use them in LORs, whenever they deem it necessary. It's their revenge on mediocre students.

Is it passive-aggressive? You betcha. But this is what the game has become. This is how some recommenders respond when they feel bullied or guilt-tripped into writing letters they don't believe in.

If professors are really writing in "code," isn't it even more important that I reserve the right to examine my letters?

First of all, don't be a student about whom secret warnings need to be transmitted. [See "How to Not Impress a Professor."]

Secondly, it may not be as simple as spotting sly innuendos in these coded LORs. Sometimes professors choose to signal lukewarm support by writing you a "merely fantastic" letter instead of the "She walks on water!" letter that they reserve for their best students. This is

I once wrote a "bad" (read: sincere) letter of recommendation soon after my arrival to the US. It was actually embellished not to reflect my utter despising for the requester, but I felt that I really owed a service to the reader. It was a true exercise in agony, trying to find the balance: I remember thinking why in the world I had been asked in the first place (I had given this person countless stern warnings about his behavior). I guess the final letter read a bit as a cautionary tale. To this day I am still considered as some kind of a bloodthirsty Kali goddess by colleagues. It was explained to me soon after how such letters are to be spelled in the US: "He does not steal as much as you would expect from a person of his hygiene." Now I get it, and have been fully absorbed into the system. But I still think it is a shame that we have to deconstruct letters looking for true meaning.
– Anonymous

---

4. *L.I.A.R.: The Lexicon of Intentionally Ambiguous Recommendations: Positive Sounding Recommendations for People Who Can't Manage Their Own Sock Drawers*, by Robert J. Thornton.

known as Being Damned by Faint Praise. Are you certain that you'd be able to recognize it?

Let's just suppose, for the sake of argument, that you refuse to sign the waiver because you want to scrutinize your LOR. In order to understand where your letter falls on the good-to-great scale, you would need to read hundreds of letters (from the current application cycle, for proper context). And then, if you realized that your letter was not up to par, your options are either to confront the prof and argue that you're far more fabulous than they described (awkward much?) or to toss the letter and start cultivating a relationship with another professor. And that's if you have the luxury of time. Chances are, your second-choice prof won't write a letter that's any better. For one thing, she doesn't know you as well as your first-choice prof—otherwise, you would have asked her first, right?

Honestly, couldn't your time be better spent improving aspects of your application that you have more control over?

The irony is that a LOR that discusses your weaknesses doesn't always hurt your application.

What do you mean?

With letter inflation as bad as it is, admissions committees can find the balanced portrayal of a student to be refreshingly real. We've heard from people who have served on admissions committees—they tell us that they're weary of the "letter inflation" phenomenon. It's kind of like grade inflation, where the average grade given in a class has crept up steadily over the years, although academic ability hasn't necessarily improved. In a LOR context, this means that adcoms are constantly struggling to figure out how good a recommendee actually is. "Great" has become standard, "good" equals a big yawn, and a neutral letter is the kiss of death. When professors support their students, they do their best to help them compete effectively in the application marketplace—and if that means puffing up the LOR, so be it. Nobody wants to put their student at a disadvantage by providing a non-inflated letter when inflation has become—quite literally—the norm. When the majority of letters are glowing, you need some pretty sophisticated shades to distinguish mere brightness from true radiance.

Many professors are also loath to write anything negative because they want to shield themselves from legal reprisal. Nobody wants to be held responsible for ruining somebody's reputation. (The higher up you get in academia, the more weight that the opinion of an advisor or research mentor has on a student's professional reputation. Recommendations carry disproportionate influence when an application process does not include face-to-face interviews, such as those for various fellowships and post-doctorate positions, as well as law school.)

I had a student who asked me, in an off-handed way, if I could write a letter for him for grad school. I said, "Sure." About a month later, I was surprised when he asked if I had written the letter. He had not given me any information about the school to which he was applying, its address, his resume, or the due date. Yet, he expected that I could just "whip one out" following his casual request.
– Dr. Jeanne Perry
UCLA

So if you're serving on an adcom and you're flooded with letters that all look the same, a very honest evaluation can really stand out. As long as the liabilities discussed in the LOR are not fatal flaws—and it definitely helps if they're paired with some context about how the applicant has worked to mitigate those weaknesses—such a letter can help admissions committees to see the applicant as a three-dimensional human being, not a generic superman. Let your recommender keep it real. It can help you!

I still think a bad LOR could take down my application!

You're not wrong about that. And there's a simple action you can take to avoid that problem. It requires you to approach this issue like the professional you want to become.

If you're afraid that your professor won't be able to recommend you "without reservation," the time to figure that out is when you request the LOR. We've said it before, and we'll say it again: Look 'em straight in the eye and ask them to be completely honest with you about whether they can write you a strong letter. (When you ask this question in the proper way, you are really saying: "Let us interact as two adults.") And professors will respond to this question quite candidly—which is what you want, isn't it? Alternately, if you're curious about whether your LOR will include a "weaknesses/room for improvement" paragraph, ask your prof straight out.

What if the professor chooses to show me the LOR she wrote for me, even after I signed the waiver?

Well, that's different. The writer of a recommendation may certainly offer to let you read a LOR.

Mind you, the key word here is "offer." They've got to volunteer it. You can't ask. The waiver you signed is basically your promise that you will never ask to read the LOR.

I'd feel so much less stressed if I knew exactly what was being written about me.

There are some who argue that the advantage presented by confidential LORs is merely anecdotal. Fair enough—it's true that you won't find any quantitative proof that non-confidential letters hold less sway with admissions officials. But you have to admit the logic of why, from the perspective of admissions committees, a confidential letter would be more trustworthy and credible.

An applicant's waiver decision sends out subtle messages about trust and confidence. First of all, admissions committees do generally assume that non-confidential letters have been read by the applicant. They also assume that most professors prefer to write confidential letters. Therefore, an applicant's insistence on reviewing his or her LORs implies either a lack of trust in their own judgment when choosing recommenders (i.e., you weren't absolutely sure

The worst for me are the "greasy" tactics where you can tell that students have read somewhere that they should visit in class, come by during your office hours, sit in the front row, etc. It is sort of written all over their face that they are, from the beginning, out to get a letter of recommendation from you. The one thing I would urge students to do is to be straight with the people they ask for letters of recommendation. It is an insult when they butter you up and you have to pretend you cannot see through that. Just be yourself and work hard. It is really simple. No amount of buttering up can substitute for that.

– Anonymous

that this prof would write you a strong letter) or a lack of trust in the recommender, period (i.e., you suspected that the prof would betray you somehow in the LOR). Neither scenario suggests an optimal teacher-student relationship. Both would give an admissions committee pause.

The application process can provoke lots of anxiety, and we do understand your temptation to exert control over this part of it. We advise you, however, to trust your recommenders. The advantage you gain in doing so may be small, but it's been our experience that most applicants will take every advantage they can get.

I'll be using the LOR credential service at my campus/department. I'm not saying I expect them to hand me a waived letter, but maybe they can give me hints about its content.

Don't count on Career Center staff to slip you any feedback on the content of your letters, either. They take the waivers very seriously, and are strictly forbidden to show confidential letters to the student, divulge specific contents, or recommend that a particular letter be used (or not) for a particular application. Sometimes, if a student is concerned that a particular LOR goes astray of its intended objective (e.g., that the letter is addressed too narrowly to certain schools or graduate programs if it was intended to be used generally), the letter service staff is allowed to review the document and inform the student whether it is appropriate for a specific purpose. You might be able to get this kind of factual confirmation from the credential service, but trying to find out anything more—including whether the recommendation is favorable—could be construed as an attempt to access a confidential file, which could theoretically lead to disciplinary action.

The fine print on my waiver form says that "no institutional service or benefit [will] be denied students who fail to supply waivers." That means admissions committees can't penalize me for sending non-confidential letters, right?

Many forms do state that your decision to waive or not waive cannot be used against you in the admissions decision-making process.

Here's another item: "Such a waiver must be voluntary and cannot be a condition of admission." Profs can't require me to sign the waiver, can they?

You are no more obligated to sign the waiver than faculty members are obligated to write you a letter of recommendation. In fact, don't be surprised if a prof refuses to write you a LOR unless you waive the right to read it. Since they're doing you a favor by writing the LOR, they can set any condition they want. This stance does not mean they have something to hide.

Actually, I want to read the letter so that I can be prepared if something from my LOR comes up in interview.

Then you will be relieved to hear that admissions personnel cannot discuss the contents of any confidential references with you, directly or by inference, in such a way that might identify the writer. They're forbidden by the same FERPA rules that prevent anybody but the author from showing you the letter. And unless you misrepresented yourself in your application or to your recommender, you shouldn't have any problems answering any questions that come up during your interview, regardless of what your recommendations say.

What if I waive access, and then change my mind later on?

Waivers can be revoked in writing (and delivered to your professor). If you do this, however, it doesn't give you the right to inspect and review documents collected while the waiver was in force.

This applies for online services as well?

Web-based services like Interfolio (www.interfolio.com) couldn't have gotten off the ground unless they could guarantee recipient institutions the same level of confidentiality provided by traditional career centers and campus dossier services. So every Interfolio client is asked to use a cover form telling their recommendation writers whether he or she is opting to make the letter confidential or non-confidential. It's essential to the process in the sense that any documents received by Interfolio without that cover form will be delayed and may even be discarded. Interfolio also requires that all confidential letters either be mailed to them in a signed envelope from the writer themselves, or be uploaded directly by the writer to their site.

Recently I was asked by a student whether I would give him the letter of recommendation so that he could make the decision whether it was good enough to send in!
– Dr. Elma Gonzalez
UCLA

Well, at least I can pick and choose certain letters in my LOR dossier to be confidential. It's not like it's all or nothing.

Not necessarily. The majority of campus letter file services, as well as Interfolio, seem to allow students to waive their access to LORs on a letter-by-letter basis. Sometimes it involves setting up two separate files—one for confidential letters, the other for non-confidential letters—but the effect is the same. However, a handful of campus/departmental LOR services play by a different set of rules. With them, it's all or nothing. By signing their Service Contract, you are agreeing to waive your rights to view all LORs that enter their possession, regardless of whether the letters are accompanied by signed waiver forms or not. Read the fine print and ask questions. Just make sure you understand all their rules before you sign up.

What are some other things I should ask about if I'm considering using a campus LOR service?

Find out: Do they require a minimum number of letters in

your file before they send it out? Do they impose a maximum number of letters that you can place in the file—perhaps even a quota on letters to a particular type of program? How long do they keep your file active, and what does it take to keep a file active? Will they destroy your letters after your file expires, or return them to the author? How much does it cost to open and maintain a file? Will they mail letters to private employers, private scholarships, private fellowships, or private grants—or only to accredited graduate programs and professional schools? Are you allowed to pick and choose which letters will be mailed out as a package? Can you retire letters from your file?

FAQ: FOLLOW UP

I know, I know … thank-you notes are common courtesy.

And sometimes they can be more—depending on when you ask for the letter. Sophomores or juniors who have earned a good letter from a professor are likely to be considered for research opportunities and undergraduate teaching assistant positions—perhaps even nominations for departmental scholarships. Even if you're a senior who's looking forward to graduating soon, don't count out the possibility that you'll need another letter from these professors in the future. In fact, that's a good rule of thumb to follow. Treat every recommender like you'll need something from him or her in the future. Neglecting to thank a recommender doesn't quite qualify as burning your bridges behind you, but it definitely creates annoyance. And the last thing you want is to have to renew a relationship with somebody who rolls their eyes when your name comes up.

Ok, I get it. But I'm a little busy right now. I'll get around to it.

Of course you will. But why don't you check right now to see if you have the cards and envelopes—just to make sure they're at hand when you're finally ready to do it. Oh, by the way—you do have the professor's address, right? You don't need to know where they live; their departmental address will do. That's easy enough, isn't it?

Well, now that you have the envelopes and the address in front of you … look, there's a pen over there. You might as well get this part over with. And the note of gratitude itself. Come to think of it, it doesn't need to be terribly complex at all, right? What's wrong with a simple message like: "Professor X, I deeply appreciate your willingness to support my application with a letter of recommendation. When I hear back from the schools I've applied to, I promise to share the news with you. Wish me luck! Sincerely, Student"

Got stamps? Of course not. Nobody ever has extra stamps at home. Maybe you should put the cards in your backpack, or by the door so you'll remember to grab them the next time you head out.

I was looking for a post-doctoral fellow for my lab, and received a good-looking CV which I decided to pursue. The applicant had only been working in their current lab for about a year, and I was therefore curious as to why they wanted to leave so soon. Luckily, the applicant's current mentor was listed as a referee at the end of the CV, so I e-mailed them to ask for a LOR. The mentor was very surprised at this enquiry, as they were not aware the person was even looking for another job. I wrote to the applicant explaining that I was not interested anymore; if a candidate is being dishonest with their current boss, they can just as easily do the same to me in a year's time. The applicant was angry with me for approaching the referee without asking him first, but I explained that everything in the CV is fair game for further investigation, and he should have been honest with his current mentor.
– Anonymous

ADVICE FOR RECOMMENDERS:
How to Write Great Letters of Recommendation

I had a PhD student who was quite talented, but his personality was awful. He was duplicitous, in constant conflict, short-tempered and just plain obnoxious. As the situation worsened, I told him that it was becoming harder and harder for me to write him a good letter.

I'm a biologist, and my students frequently conduct their research with NIH funding. These funds have basic requirements and specific codes of misconduct. The PhD student finally did graduate. As soon as we signed off on his dissertation, he disappeared, taking all of his data with him (making it impossible to publish his work). We still don't know why he did this—to be spiteful? But a later email gave me the distinct impression that he was going to pull a "you'll get my data back if you write a good letter." (It is a given that PhD students need good letters from their mentors. If such letters are not supportive, they face a very difficult road).

Removal of data collected with NIH funds results in the loss of thousands of tax dollars and years of work—and is classified as misconduct. This incident is now under investigation by our office of research and integrity, and will go on to NIH. This will result in sanctions, such as the removal of all funding and ineligibility for future grants for the next 5–10 years... which literally will destroy the career of a developing scientist, because you usually need to get funding to get tenure. This likely will happen to my former student, making six years of education and training useless, and ruining his career. Meanwhile, I lost two years of good work, several publications, and thousands of NIH dollars. So everybody lost out in this little stunt.

You may have to tell students that, while a letter may be agreed upon, blackmailing your mentor to get a good one will get you nowhere!
– Anonymous

PREAMBLE: REMIND ME AGAIN WHY I WRITE THESE LETTERS

1. You couldn't have risen to your current position without letters of recommendation. You're grateful to mentors and supervisors who gave you a boost, and you want to pass it on.

2. When committees make admissions decisions, they can decide pretty quickly which candidates fall into the "Definitely Accept" and "Definitely Reject" piles. The vast majority of applications fall somewhere in the middle. Some schools rely heavily on recommenders' evaluations to whittle down that middle pile.

3. In situations where the vast majority of LORs are positive (letter inflation), adcoms are more likely to peruse letters of recommendation for red flags that than to use letters as predictors of an applicant's performance. When letters are read primarily for the purpose of screening out unsuitable applicants, the omission of particular subjects can lead to the interpretation of the letter-writer's general evaluation as unfavorable.

4. Admissions committees often look to recommenders to validate and verify the claims that applicants make in their application essays.

5. Admissions committees need to know how likely a student will be to successfully transition into the next phase of their academic or professional lives. A star student in high school is probably prepared to handle the increased rigor and independence of college work, but there are always exceptions; likewise, it is by no means guaranteed that everybody who excels as an undergraduate will be able to gracefully negotiate the quantum leap into graduate school or the working world. An experienced recommender will be able to tease out the traits that promote present achievement from those that portend future success—and highlight them in the letter.

6. Your words have the power to transform the candidate from a stick figure into an oil portrait—a fleshed-out, memorable individual.

7. The warmth of your tone in the LOR provides clues about the applicant's interpersonal skills.

8. The applicant's decision to choose you to author this evaluation reveals much about his or her judgment.

9. Each letter that you write makes the next one easier. After all, given the demands on your time, nobody expects you to write a LOR *de novo* for each applicant. In fact, by working from your personal LOR template, you help facilitate the comparisons that admissions decision-makers need to make. When possible, adcoms compare letters from the same recommender; significant variations in language help them determine which candidate is more highly regarded.

10. You can say things about the applicants that they cannot say themselves.

FAQ: LEGAL ISSUES

I'm new at writing recommendations. I hear that there's a lot of legal issues to keep in mind.[5]

Some people have complained that writing LORs nowadays with any degree of candor is like facing down a minefield. Considering the legal issues that can arise around the issues of confidentiality, privacy and liability for defamation, a certain degree of caution is justifiable. Generally speaking, however, LOR content can be safely negotiated if you blanket the process with enough release forms.

Keep two things in mind. First of all, it's illegal to mention protected status. In order to comply with federal anti-discrimination laws, you should resist any temptation to identify—directly or indirectly—the candidate's race, color, gender (beyond the unavoidable use of the pronouns "he" and "she"), religion, age, physical or mental disability, marital status, sexual orientation, national origin, citizenship, medical condition, or political affiliations, beliefs or activities.

(Blindingly obvious? Of course. But it's always nice to get a refresher course when legalities are involved. Along those lines, here's another self-evident truth: if you display a pattern of preference for individuals belonging to certain groups—e.g., you consistently rate

---

5. None of the information or advice in this chapter should be taken as legal advice. We are not legal professionals. If you are concerned about potential liability in regards to writing recommendations or references, your first step should be to contact your institution's legal counsel, to accurately assess your rights and options under federal law as well as the most up-to-date laws and regulations in your state and industry.

them more highly than individuals of other groups, or you agree to write letters or serve as reference only for certain individuals, based upon their race, age, sex, national origin, disability, or religion—you leave yourself open to charges of discrimination.)

Alright, I get it: Discrimination is bad. What else?

And then there's FERPA. The Family Education Rights and Privacy Act was passed in 1974 to give students the discretion to decide how much of their educational record may be disclosed by university employees to third parties. FERPA defines "educational record" broadly to include any records, files or documents maintained by the university that contain information directly related to a student. So in other words, you are technically required to get the student's specific written permission to discuss practically anything relating to their college career in a letter or verbal reference.[6]

When you say "practically anything" …

The exceptions are a few bare-bones items, known as Directory Information. In FERPA-speak, the term "Directory Information" refers to information that would not be considered harmful or an invasion of privacy if it were disclosed. (Of course, students have the right to restrict even Directory Information from being given out—a decision that can complicate matters significantly, as we'll discuss briefly later.)

We would love to provide a definitive list of items that can be divulged freely, but educational institutions vary significantly in regards to the types of information they protect. They differ because state laws regarding the privacy of student records are occasionally even more restrictive than FERPA, and of course, individual colleges and universities may choose to be even more stringent than that.

This means that it's incumbent upon you, the LOR writer or reference-giver, to find out exactly how your educational institution currently defines Directory Information. The more restrictive their definition, the more likely you are to need permission to discuss non-Directory Information.

We've compiled a chart to give you an idea of the range of "personally identifiable" student information that various universities

When I was an undergrad, I was looking for people to write me letters for graduate school. Most faculty who I asked said sure. However, one faculty member, who later won a Nobel prize, looked at my record and told me no. I was stunned as this was a professor with whom I had taken one lower division class and two upper division classes in my major, earning an A, an A-, and a B+. I had also worked in his research lab one summer. He explained that at the better schools I was applying to (MIT, University of Chicago, UC Berkeley, etc.) I would be borderline based on my record, and he didn't want his letter to be the deciding factor on whether I got in or not. He didn't think I had done well enough to be successful at these schools and he didn't want that to reflect badly on him.
– Dr. Jeff Saul
Florida International University

---

6. Here's some relevant advice:
"Statements made by a recommender which are made from the recommender's personal observation or knowledge do not require a written release from the student who is the subject of the recommendation. However, if personally identifiable information from the student's educational record is included in a letter of recommendation (grades, GPA, etc.), the writer is required to obtain a signed release from the students which 1) specifies the records that may be disclosed, 2) states the purpose of the disclosure, 3) identifies the party or class of parties to whom the disclosure can be made, and 4) is signed and dated by the student."

Adapted from *Guidelines for Postsecondary Institutions for Implementation of the Family Educational Rights and Privacy Act of 1974 as Amended*, Revised Edition 1998, Richard A. Rainsberger, American Association of Collegiate Registrars and Admissions Officers.

HOW STRICTLY DOES YOUR UNIVERSITY INTERPRET FERPA?

Almost always included in Directory Information; does not require student's authorization	Personally Identifiable Information that is sometimes classified as Directory Information; may require the student's authorization	Never included in Directory Information; always requires the student's authorization

Student's Full Name
Academic Status
   (Undergraduate, Graduate,
   General Studies)
Dates of attendance
Degrees Completed
	Student's address (local and permanent)
	Telephone listing
	Email address (campus and/or other addresses)
	Photographs
	Parents' names and addresses/emergency contact
	Date and place of birth
	Marital status
	Residency status
	Religious affiliation
	Sexual orientation
	Records relating to a student's disability and
	    accommodations provided for that disability
	The most recent educational institution attended
	Participation in officially recognized activities and sports
	Weight and height (if member of an athletic team)
	Degrees, honors, and awards received
	Major/minor field of study
	Candidacy for degree
	Graduation status (i.e., un-met degree requirements)
	Dates of degrees
	Grade level/class standing
	Cumulative academic credit hours earned
	Academic transcripts (official or unofficial)
	Current class schedule or enrollment information
	GPA
	Class rank
	Grades/exam scores
	Standardized test scores (e.g., SAT, GRE, MCAT)
	Academic standing (e.g., probation; suspension;
	    petitions; readmit)
	Fees paid; financial aid and billing information
	Student employment records (if employed as graduate
	    teaching or research assistant, his/her campus address
	    and office hours)
	General assessment of performance of student in a class or
	    in a field-based experience
	Advising conference notes
	Residence hall information
	Internships and field placement records
	"performance indicators"
	"any list of personal characteristics or other information that
	    would make the student's identity traceable"
	"any reference to progress or deficiencies"
		Student identification number
		Student PIN numbers
		Social security numbers
		Ethnicity
		Race
		Nationality
		Class schedule/class location

have cautioned their faculty not to casually discuss. Notice how much of it is information that one would assume "belongs" in a LOR, or would naturally arise in a conversation with a potential employer.

That's pretty restrictive! A LOR that limited itself to divulging only Directory Information wouldn't be much of a recommendation at all.

Of course, common sense does apply here. You should be able to comment on grades that you gave or classroom performance that you have personally observed. Any information that has been provided to you by the student (e.g., resume or personal statement) is also generally considered fair game, but in our opinion, it is definitely in your best interest to require your students to fill out and sign a Reference Release Form. It is often combined with the form where students are asked if they want to waive their right to read your LOR. If your university doesn't already have a standard form, take a look at the template we've included on p. 36 and adapt it for your own purposes.

We've even seen a few forms that release the referee from any liability, e.g., *"I release Acme University, its employees and the person(s) providing the above described reference or evaluation from all claims and liability for damages that may result from their compliance with this request."* If you're a prof who despairs over "LOR inflation"—if you long to be more candid in your letters about the candidates' weaknesses—you may want to consider including this extra little codicil on the Reference Release Form that you provide to your students.

Regardless, the further you venture from what your institution has defined as Directory Information, the more advisable it is that you get the student's written consent; it will free you to write the superbly comprehensive LOR that was your intention all along. For example, if you feel that your letter would be incomplete if it does not discuss some obstacle the student has surmounted—and which would necessitate revealing some protected category—you really must cover your bases. Insist that the student specifically authorize you in their reference release form to mention those topics.

But in my day, I never signed off on these items, and I know that my profs discussed my GPA or my weaknesses in the LORs they wrote for me.

Times sure have changed, haven't they?

I hardly think that my students will come back and sue me for revealing their GPA or grades in a LOR, especially since I'd be praising their academic abilities.

Life is unpredictable, and the Reference Release Form is a simple, pre-emptive step. As insurance policies go, this is a cheap one.

If you want more information about FERPA, this site is a great place to learn about the federal legislation: http://www.aacrao.

org/ferpa_guide/enhanced/main_frameset.html. Of course, you should always check with your university's registrar or office of legal counsel to stay up-to-date on the policies implemented to safeguard the privacy of students at your particular institution.

———————

FERPA rules still apply to students' records after they graduate, right?

Yes. No matter how long ago a student graduated, any letters of recommendation or verbal references provided on their behalf would be subject to the same privacy restrictions that pertained when they were still enrolled. FERPA protects all personally identifiable information collected while a student is attending the educational institution—and the guarantee of confidentiality is supposed to remain in effect until the student revokes it in writing. The only difference is that post-graduation information about the student (e.g., alumni records) is not considered part of their educational record.

———————

I've also heard that professors are better off identifying the letter as a "reference" rather than a "recommendation" if it contains any criticism at all.

Although some faculty members insist on making the distinction as a point of personal integrity, it's just as likely that their interest in precise language is motivated by a desire to protect themselves legally. Indeed, we can report that the legal counsel for certain universities even go so far as to advise that professors get the student to acknowledge (with another signed release) that the professor is writing them a letter of reference (or evaluation) instead of a letter of recommendation. Although the semantic distinction does have the virtue of clarity, you must decide for yourself whether the extra red tape is worth it.

———————

Speaking of references … I'm a professor whose students often go straight into the work world, so I'm asked to be a reference (both verbally and in writing) as often as I get requests for academic letters of recommendation.

Before you say anything to an employer about a student, make sure you have, at minimum: 1) the student's confirmation that you are named as an official reference on the employment application or resume; and 2) the student's signed statement authorizing you to discuss their educational information. Ideally, you've also discussed with the student what you'd say in the reference. This last point is crucial. Forewarned is forearmed.

Early on in my career of LOR writing, a pre-med student asked me for a copy of his recommendation, and I provided it to him. Many years later, one of his peers confided in me: the recommendee had written his own letter, then literally cut and pasted it between my letterhead and signature. This was a lesson for me! I no longer give out my letters. I will let students come to my office and read the letters but I never give out hard copies or electronic copies.
– Dr. Jeanne Perry
UCLA

In most states, employers who write letters of reference for job-seekers are protected by job reference immunity legislation. Because most professors are not in the position of directly employing their students, the written and verbal references that faculty members provide are not protected by statutory law. In the event that any of your students decide that your statements are false, have tangibly harmed their reputation and lowered their esteem within the community, your defense against their claims of defamation would have to rest instead on common law principles: namely, that your statements were unimpeachably true and accurate, and that they were protected by qualified privilege. "Qualified privilege" applies to statements made in good faith, which are directed solely to people who have a legitimate interest in the subject, and which disclose information necessary to serve their legitimate interest in an employee's fitness to perform.

When you speak or write as a reference, following these general rules will keep you from crossing the line into the Land of Liability. Never fax or email an employment reference. Let the potential employer lead the conversation; instead of volunteering information, you should answer his or her specific inquiries and only verify facts that you have personal knowledge of. Don't make guesses or engage in speculation. If you veer into the realm of personal opinion, make that shift very clear to the potential employer—and be able to back your opinions up with specific incidents. Lastly, there is no such thing as "off the record."

———————————

Wait a sec—some students direct the university to keep even their Directory Information under wraps. If I'm listed as a reference for one of those students, and some would-be employer calls me up to ask about him, I'd have to explain why I couldn't say anything about that student, right?

Actually, the legal Möbius strip goes further than that. If you know that a student has filed a Request to Restrict Directory Information (a.k.a. a "FERPA block"), you—as a university employee—are not even allowed to acknowledge that he or she is, or has ever been, a student at the school. The safest reply would be something to the effect of: "I have no comment regarding the individual you are referring to." Or that old chestnut, beloved of diplomats everywhere: "I can neither confirm nor deny." (Congratulations! You've just bent over backwards, made a half-twist, and grabbed your own toes.) In such a situation, we would suggest ending the conversation as quickly as possible by referring the information-seeker to your university's registrar. Afterwards, you would be completely justified in admonishing the student, who presumably listed you as a reference, for putting you in such an impossible position.

As a manager, what should I know about providing references for former employees? I've been told that I can get into legal trouble if I write a too-candid description of an employee who was difficult. Do I have to disclose negative information about these individuals?

In most states, employers who write letters of reference for job-seekers are protected by job reference immunity legislation. Not only are you free to disclose negative information about your former employee [providing that the statements are: 1) an evaluation by a qualified supervisor, 2) specific to the job in question, 3) divulged only to the prospective employer, 4) not motivated by "malice or reckless disregard for the truth or falsity of the information provided," and most importantly, 5) true—in other words, its accuracy is verifiable], but you're actually obligated to do so if you honestly believe the employee's background suggests that he or she is unfit for the position and could potentially cause harm to others. Failing to mention potentially harmful behaviors is a form of misrepresentation, and it's called Negligent Referral.

All this talk may be enough to put you off writing letters of reference completely, and you are certainly within your rights to decline these requests. You have no legal obligation to provide references or recommendations. (Although there's even been some debate about whether, in some circumstances, the act of refusing to write a letter for individuals who pose a "substantial, foreseeable risk of harm" would constitute actionable negligence; after all, remaining silent is another form of being less than truthful and forthcoming.) That's why so many states have passed legislation to give reference-writers the latitude to be completely candid about their former employees. And employers who live in states without job reference immunity statutes can take heart in knowing that the courts already provide them some cover; generally speaking, state case law provides immunity to employers who disclose information in good faith.

Isn't there that one sentence that you're supposed to include in all employment letters of reference to protect yourself legally?

You mean this one? "This information is confidential, should be treated as such, and is provided at the request of [name of student or applicant], who has asked me to serve as a reference." (Or other language to that effect.)

Yes, by providing justification for the communication, such statements leave no doubt that the information was not given to hurt a person's reputation. One final note: It's also a good idea to require the individuals seeking a letter of reference/recommendation to make their requests in writing; this documentation—which should be kept on file for at least three years—is evidence of their consent that your statements be published (i.e., communicated to a third party).

FAQ: MANAGING BORDERLINE/UNRECOMMENDABLE RECOMMENDEES

I'm at such a loss when students who earned a C+ in my class ask me for a letter.

Let me guess: it happens every year like an agonizing ritual. Students whom you have never seen before in your life suddenly appear in your office. Some of them smile painfully; others plunge quickly into their script. "I loved your class! I really liked that one lecture on stereoisomers/Charlotte Brönte/deficit finance," they assure you. "I understood all the material, but I just couldn't seem to pull it together for the exams. Um, so I was wondering? If you'd write me a recommendation…?" If your teaching load includes many undergraduates, it's almost inevitable that some percentage of the LOR requests you receive will feel impossible to fulfill.

You don't have to live like this. There is a solution. The strategy we suggest is not radically new by any means, but it is effective.

Plan ahead, and set expectations upfront: inform students at the outset that you refuse to write letters for anybody who earns below a grade of X in your class, or anybody who gives you less than Y amount of advance notice. You can even specify that you need to see Z materials from them before you give your final answer.

You are the one setting the terms, so think back on which LOR requests you have, in the past, been happy to entertain—the ones that truly deserved your time and attention. Be honest with yourself about what you want and what you need. Then make it clear to students that you will accept nothing less. Be strict or lenient, as you prefer. But be clear. If you mandate that students must have earned a B or higher in your class in order to approach you for a recommendation, caution them that they must still ask you this question: "Would you be able to write me a strong letter of recommendation?" Perhaps even more important, coach them to be prepared for your honest answer.

Many professors who adopt this "upfront" strategy never again have to write a mediocre letter of recommendation. We know of one professor who offers a variation on this theme. He tells students that his letters only come in two flavors: strong or worthless. The former are enthusiastic and filled with detailed anecdotes. The latter look like this:

To Whom It May Concern:

John Student took my class in Winter of 200x and received a grade of B-.

Sincerely,
Professor Recommender

Here's the key part. When we say "upfront," we mean: 1) Spell out these expectations on your syllabi (and course websites), and 2) Discuss them on the first day of class.

Spread the word about your new rules. Develop a reputation. Don't make exceptions unless you're willing to make subsequent exceptions. It really is that simple.

Admittedly, this strategy—which is based on giving students a fair amount of advance warning—doesn't work retroactively. So you'll still have to deal with students from the recent (and distant!) past coming out of the woodwork making unreasonable, plaintive demands. But the sooner you institute this rule, the sooner you can embark on your saner LOR life. Imagine writing letters only for students whom you honestly believe have a good shot at winning acceptance to grad school. Imagine having enough time (and the supplemental materials) to do a proper job. It's possible, but it won't happen on its own.

We've heard from several professors who have instituted rules in this fashion, and they report far fewer headaches since they drew a line in the sand.

Urgh! Why does this even happen?

Your question is rhetorical. You already know the answer.

What makes things awkward is when LOR seekers and LOR writers negotiate under assumptions or out of wishful thinking (see next page). It's a recipe for codependence.

LOR codependence results when the student's desperation and deadline anxiety encounters a recommender's unwillingness to play the bad guy. The student displays a neediness that is self-abasing and overwhelming. The professor puts up resistance, but soon finds that logical arguments (e.g., "My letter will actually hurt your application.") don't seem to penetrate. Finally, he or she gives in, feeling a mixture of guilt, irritation and rancor. Everybody feels helpless.

The professor who agrees to write a letter for an unqualified student then faces the discomfort of living up to obligations that he or she doesn't believe in. When you spin the truth by coming up with inventive euphemisms for underwhelming applicants, do you ever feel like your integrity is being compromised somehow? You're not the first professor to think so.

Unless you suffer from a pathological desire to be loved by all your students, adopting the "upfront" strategy should be eminently feasible. You may have had trouble saying "no" in the past, but this strategy is tailor-made for you. The act of denying requests is made easier when you've warned students from the beginning that "no" was a definite possibility. And from the student's perspective, hearing "no" won't be so bad if they truly understand it as your prerogative—that a LOR is a privilege that they earn, not an entitlement associated with

LOR CODEPENDENCY: THE SIGNS AND SYMPTOMS

ASSUMPTIONS

APPLICANT	RECOMMENDER
Without a full set of LORs, my application will be incomplete. This prof is my last (or only) hope, so I'll take anything from him or her—even a mediocre letter.	Nobody's dumb enough to sabotage their application with a mediocre letter.
Writing LORs is part of their job. Why else am I paying all this of money to be provided an education?	Since I'm doing this person a favor, both common courtesy and common sense would dictate that they approach me—and the process—with a modicum of respect.
The prof's really down-to-earth and approachable. He won't mind if I jot him a quick note to request a LOR.	Surely they realize that this is the first step of the rest of their lives. Surely they realize that unprofessional behavior leaves a bad taste.
Writing a LOR can't really be that complicated. When I'm requesting a transcript, I only need to give the registrar a few days notice—a LOR won't take that much more time, right?	I'm not comfortable putting my name on a form letter. If I commit to writing a letter, I'm going to make an effort to personalize it, which I can't do if the applicant doesn't provide me with adequate information about his or her application.

WISHFUL THINKING

APPLICANT	RECOMMENDER
I wish my prof would make a special effort to put my B- in the best possible light.	I wish that only my best, most deserving students would ask for letters.
I wish my prof would put this letter at the top of his priority list because I need it right away!	I wish they could truly appreciate how busy I am.
I wish my prof understood that I don't think this letter will make much of a difference at all.	I wish all students understood how seriously I take the letter-writing process.
I wish my prof understood how much of my application is based on magical thinking—and would therefore just play along by whipping out a letter ASAP.	

enrolling in your class. In fact, setting this contract with students is actually an empowering gesture. You are educating students about how much control they have over the behaviors leading up to your "Yes, I'd be happy to" or "No, I'm sorry."

So go towards the win-win. Walk towards clarity. Quash assumptions before they have a chance to grow into a sense of entitlement. The beauty of this approach is that it will not seem unfair to students at the time that they hear it (i.e., on the first day of class), but they will be bound by it anyway. No student starts off plotting to inconvenience you by asking for a LOR at the last minute; no one says to themselves: "I think I'll perform indifferently in this class AND ask this professor to support my future application." LOR frustration happens when students realize too late that their options are limited. Therefore, establishing a contract with them is an easy, early ounce of prevention. Yes, this is just one more thing you have to educate your students about. But you're an educator. Haven't you already established a contract with your students in the form of your syllabus (i.e., I will teach you this knowledge, drawing upon these sources, and evaluate your performance in this way)? Just add one more item to that contract.

OK, I'm willing to believe that this "tough love" advice would probably work on undergrads—or at least make the situation better. But how about writing letters for difficult grad students or post-docs? The stakes are even higher because letters from advisors, committee members, or research supervisors can literally make or break a graduate student's career.

First, let's look on the bright side. Graduate students have all gone through the LOR process at least once, which means they're familiar with the mechanics of preparing their recommenders. Moreover, because it's understood from the get-go that they'll need good letters to advance further in their career (i.e., building relationships with mentors is as crucial to their professionalization as attending conferences, publishing articles, and networking), they have stronger motivation to do good work. The ideal relationship, obviously, is one in which advisees receive candid, constructive feedback about whether their work is up to par long before they need the LOR. Proactive advising is the best way to avoid situations where the faculty member is—once again—reduced to the act of couching warnings and red flags to LOR readers in clever, nuanced prose.

Given all these built-in mechanisms for communication and interaction, your problem is not about writing a recommendation based on inadequate information. If anything, you understand far too intimately the tendency of a young post-doc to spend her bench time chatting rather than working, or the work habits of a grad student who has never turned in a paper on time. Your dilemma is trying to provide a truly candid assessment of the applicant's capacity for advanced work without being held liable for costing the student a desired position.

We hew to the same advice: Frank talk goes down easier when it comes early.

The perfect time to lay down the law is during new student orientation. Blunt do's and don'ts work fine—during their first few weeks, grad students are as receptive and amenable as they'll ever be. Using 3rd person stories is a great way to outline your values and expectations without implying that the people in front of you are ignorant. (If you don't have any tales of your own, feel free to borrow some of the following horror stories …) Convey your LOR rules as a parable or cautionary tale if that approach appeals to you, but do it as early as possible, and reinforce it in writing.

FAQ: VARIATIONS ON THE BASIC LOR

I am a literature professor, and one of my students just asked me to write a LOR for their application to medical school.

If you are recommending Applicant Surname for a Program or Institution that feels academically foreign to you, don't fret about the cross-disciplinary gap. Professional schools or Prestigious Programs that require their applicants to submit LORs from a diverse range of backgrounds want to filter out candidates who are too narrowly focused; they want students who have the intellectual flexibility to impress professors of all academic backgrounds. So do as you would for any other letter. Studio art professors accustomed to evaluating student work for creativity, technique, originality and/or eloquence of expression would add breadth to the application of a dental or veterinary hopeful by emphasizing those traits in their letters; likewise, primary investigators who rate young researchers on a checklist of traits such as quantitative aptitude, problem-solving ability, perseverance, ability to follow protocol can assure law or business school admissions committees that the applicant possesses analytical rigor. All of these traits are broadly appropriate. However, you may also want to consult the discipline-specific checklists listed later in this chapter.

I should cut back on the academic details if I'm writing an employment letter of reference, right?

Potential employers are interested in the same category of traits as are graduate schools—general intellectual excellence as reflected in a student's aptitude for absorbing, synthesizing, and applying knowledge; in this sense, a LOR written for an employment situation need not differ much at all. Employers, however, may be especially interested in what you have to say about Applicant Surname's work ethic and tenacity, time management skills, ability to lead and work with others, and oral communication skills. If you had extensive one-on-one conversations with Applicant, comment on what those interactions suggested about his relationship with authority—for example, that he was admirably amenable to suggestions, or that he was quite an independent thinker. If you had occasion to observe the Applicant's ability to handle conflict, pressure and deadlines, you would be doing potential employers a big favor by rating those skills as well.

I'm sponsoring a student's proposal for a research grant. Any tips?

If you are supporting Applicant Surname's proposal for project funding, you should indicate in your letter the intellectual and logistical support that Mr. Surname could expect from you, should he be awarded the monies, as well as how much time you are prepared to commit to supervising their independent study project. Talk about his potential to contribute new knowledge to the field. Here is also where you reference your own track record in recommending/sponsoring undergraduates, if this letter is personalized for a particular Institution or Program (as opposed to slightly generic because it will be sent to several/read by more than one admissions committee). Citing previous applicant (by name, when possible) who successfully applied for that Program assists the readers in making a concrete basis for comparison; moreover, it burnishes your standing as a recommender who knows how to pick 'em. A perspicacious mentor who can spot and nurture potential stars.

CHECKLISTS OF QUALITIES DESIRED BY VARIOUS INSTITUTIONS AND PROFESSIONAL DISCIPLINES

Many letter-writers find themselves at a loss when they are asked to recommend applicants for programs or disciplines dissimilar to their own professional background. They worry that the targeted skills and abilities that they usually draw attention to may not be the ones that the LOR reader will find most relevant—and therefore, that the utility of their LOR will be diminished in the admissions process. In the next few pages, we catalogue the intellectual and social qualities that various admissions and hiring committees most value in their applicants (the indented items break down the main traits into more specific skill-sets). Although an ideal applicant would possess all of these qualities to some degree, the letter-writer should not feel obligated to cover them all in any single letter.

CHECKLIST OF QUALITIES DESIRED IN COLLEGE APPLICANTS

- ☐ Academic Preparation
    - ☐ Academic achievement relative to others of the same age and academic level
    - ☐ Classroom contribution
    - ☐ Analytical ability
    - ☐ Enthusiasm for intellectual pursuits
    - ☐ Research aptitude
    - ☐ Creativity/imagination
    - ☐ Academic focus
- ☐ Initiative and Motivation
- ☐ Ability to Work with Others
    - ☐ Potential for leadership
    - ☐ Ability to work in teams
- ☐ Interpersonal Skills
- ☐ Perseverance in Pursuing Goals
    - ☐ Self-reliance and independence
    - ☐ Reaction to adversity
    - ☐ Disciplined work habits
    - ☐ Success in completing long-range assignments with a minimum of supervision
- ☐ Effectiveness in Writing
- ☐ Effectiveness in Speaking
- ☐ Emotional Maturity
- ☐ Overall Potential for Growth

CHECKLIST OF QUALITIES DESIRED IN APPLICANTS TO GRADUATE PROGRAMS

- □ Motivation for Advanced Study
  - □ Academic focus
  - □ Long-term commitment
  - □ Suitability for subsequent practice in the profession
- □ Intellectual Preparation for Graduate Work
  - □ Academic achievement relative to others of the same age and academic level
  - □ Capacity for critical reasoning and logical analysis
  - □ Depth and breadth of knowledge in his or her major field
  - □ Intellectual curiosity/love for learning
  - □ Ability to manage a rigorous academic workload
  - □ Consistency of performance
  - □ Extenuating circumstances that might account for atypical grade(s) or course load(s)
- □ Research Skills
  - □ Ability to undertake and successfully complete a major project
  - □ Diligence and self-discipline
  - □ Resourcefulness, patience and attention to detail
  - □ Familiarity with research methodologies and techniques
- □ Potential for Future Scholarship/Creative Endeavor
  - □ Divergent thinking and creative imagination
  - □ Intellectual independence
- □ Ethical Standards & Integrity
- □ Maturity and Emotional Stability
  - □ Personal characteristics that might either help or hinder the applicant's development
- □ Oral English Expression Skills
- □ Written English Expression Skills
  - □ Ability to organize and express ideas clearly
- □ Interpersonal Effectiveness
  - □ Ability to work with others
- □ Potential as a Teacher
  - □ Ability to assess other people's strengths and liabilities
  - □ Ability to lead and motivate others
- □ Overall Promise

CHECKLIST OF QUALITIES DESIRED IN APPLICANTS TO MEDICAL SCHOOL AND ALLIED HEALTH PROGRAMS

- ☐ Motivation for a Career in Health Care
  - ☐ Realistic understanding of the day-to-day realities of working as a health professional
  - ☐ Firsthand experience in healthcare settings
  - ☐ Knowledge of the current issues in healthcare delivery and medical ethics
  - ☐ Career focus and long-term goals
- ☐ Maturity
  - ☐ Reliability
  - ☐ Integrity
  - ☐ Life experience
- ☐ Intellectual Readiness
  - ☐ Academic achievement relative to others from the same college or university
  - ☐ Ability to deal with complex and abstract ideas
  - ☐ Ability to work independently
  - ☐ Consistency of performance
  - ☐ Ability to manage a rigorous academic workload
  - ☐ Extenuating circumstances that might account for atypical grade(s) or course load(s)
  - ☐ Intellectual curiosity/love for learning
- ☐ Research Experience
  - ☐ Laboratory skills and techniques
- ☐ Judgment
  - ☐ Decision-making skills
  - ☐ Critical reasoning
  - ☐ Analytical skills
  - ☐ Problem-solving skills
- ☐ Perseverance
  - ☐ Long-term commitment
  - ☐ Ability to negotiate obstacles and setbacks
  - ☐ Self-discipline
- ☐ Emotional Stability
  - ☐ Positive attitude
  - ☐ Self-confidence
- ☐ Values/Character
  - ☐ Ethical behavior
  - ☐ Compassion
  - ☐ Empathy
  - ☐ Altruism
  - ☐ Humility
- ☐ Service to Others
  - ☐ Community-based volunteer work
  - ☐ Relevant employment experiences
- ☐ Interpersonal Skills
  - ☐ Teamwork
  - ☐ Leadership skills
  - ☐ Oral communication skills
  - ☐ Written communication skills
- ☐ Tolerance
  - ☐ Multicultural awareness and sensitivity
- ☐ Overall Potential

CHECKLIST OF QUALITIES DESIRED IN LAW SCHOOL APPLICANTS

- ☐ Motivation for a Career in Law
  - ☐ Realistic understanding of the day-to-day realities of working as a lawyer
  - ☐ Knowledge of the current issues in law and legal ethics
  - ☐ Career focus
  - ☐ Long-term goals
- ☐ Maturity
  - ☐ Reliability
  - ☐ Trustworthiness
  - ☐ Integrity
  - ☐ Life experience
- ☐ Research Skills
  - ☐ Ability to undertake and successfully complete a major project
  - ☐ Resourcefulness, patience and attention to detail
- ☐ Intellectual Qualifications
  - ☐ Academic achievement relative to others from the same college or university
  - ☐ Ability to write and speak with clarity, precision, and efficiency
  - ☐ Ability to read and listen carefully for fine points and subtle distinctions
  - ☐ Well-developed analytical skills (especially to form and defend balanced opinions)
  - ☐ Ability to juggle multiple variables
  - ☐ Prospensity for legal reasoning (deductive reasoning, inductive reasoning, and reasoning by analogy)
  - ☐ Ability to think independently
  - ☐ Ability to distinguish the relevant from the extraneous
  - ☐ Tolerance for ambiguity (ability to recognize exceptions and qualifications which may modify general rules)
  - ☐ Intellectual curiosity
  - ☐ Ability to pose pertinent questions
  - ☐ Extenuating circumstances that might account for atypical grade(s) or course load(s)
- ☐ Perseverance
  - ☐ Long-term commitment
  - ☐ Ability to negotiate obstacles and setbacks
  - ☐ Self-discipline
  - ☐ Reliability
- ☐ Interpersonal Communication Skills
  - ☐ Expository skills
  - ☐ Negotiation and persuasion skills
  - ☐ Leadership abilities inside and outside the classroom
- ☐ Potential to Successfully Adjust to the Rigors of Law School
  - ☐ Initiative to manage competitive pressure of large classes
  - ☐ Diligence, organization and time management to master substantial amounts of material
- ☐ Overall Potential

CHECKLIST OF QUALITIES DESIRED IN BUSINESS SCHOOL APPLICANTS

- ☐ Motivation for Pursuing a Career in Business
  - ☐ Realistic understanding of the day-to-day realities of working in his or her chosen field
  - ☐ Career Focus and long-term goals
- ☐ Analytical Ability
- ☐ Communication Skills
  - ☐ Negotiation and persuasion skills
  - ☐ Ability to write in a clear, effective and well-organized manner
- ☐ Intellectual Readiness
  - ☐ Academic achievement relative to others from the same college or university
  - ☐ Ability to deal with complex and abstract ideas
  - ☐ Consistency of performance
  - ☐ Ability to handle a rigorous academic workload
  - ☐ Extenuating circumstances that might account for atypical grade(s) or course load(s)
  - ☐ Intellectual curiosity/love for learning
- ☐ Emotional Maturity
  - ☐ Professionalism
  - ☐ Ability to negotiate challenges and setbacks
  - ☐ Mature attitude towards failure
  - ☐ Self-discipline
  - ☐ Willingness to accept constructive criticism
- ☐ Self-knowledge
  - ☐ Insight into his or her own assets and liabilities
- ☐ Leadership Skills/Managerial Potential
  - ☐ Ability to assess other people's strengths and liabilities
  - ☐ Ability to effectively delegate responsibility
  - ☐ Ability to motivate others
- ☐ Interpersonal Skills
  - ☐ Ability to understand other's viewpoints
  - ☐ Aptitude for social networking
  - ☐ Success in working on teams
- ☐ Assertiveness
  - ☐ Competitiveness
  - ☐ Self-confidence
  - ☐ Initiative
  - ☐ Aptitude for creating opportunities
- ☐ Ethical Integrity
- ☐ Track Record of Successfully Accomplishing Objectives
  - ☐ Project management skills
  - ☐ Time management skills
  - ☐ Problem-solving skills
- ☐ Creativity
  - ☐ Resourcefulness
- ☐ Ability to operate effectively in cultural environments other than his/her own
- ☐ Overall Potential

CHECKLIST OF QUALITIES DESIRED IN EMPLOYEES

- ☐ Intelligence
  - ☐ Analytical skills
  - ☐ Problem-solving skills
  - ☐ Ability to assimilate, retain, and apply new information
- ☐ Willingness to Accept Responsibility
  - ☐ Accountability
- ☐ Initiative
  - ☐ Ability to accomplish tasks without direct supervision
  - ☐ Track record of successfully accomplishing objectives
- ☐ Professional Self-Presentation
- ☐ Maturity
  - ☐ Ability to handle challenges and setbacks
  - ☐ Willingness to accept constructive criticism
  - ☐ Willingness to admit mistakes and ask for help when needed
- ☐ Self-Confidence
  - ☐ Energy level
  - ☐ Positive attitude
- ☐ Interpersonal Skills
  - ☐ Customer service orientation
  - ☐ Verbal communication skills
  - ☐ Writing ability
  - ☐ Persuasive skills
- ☐ Understanding of Job and Industry
  - ☐ Appropriate vocational skills
- ☐ Ability to Work Under Pressure
  - ☐ Time management skills
- ☐ Leadership
  - ☐ Aptitude for managing others
- ☐ Teamwork
  - ☐ Ability to manage and resolve conflicts
- ☐ Commitment to Company
  - ☐ Suitability of medium- or long-term goals with current position
- ☐ Creativity
  - ☐ Imagination
  - ☐ Flexibility/adaptability

ADVICE FOR GHOSTWRITERS:
How to Draft Great Letters of Recommendation

I am on the graduate admissions committee for a science department at a large public university. A couple of years back, I received a letter of recommendation from a professor on behalf of a student who was applying to our Ph.D. program. This student was in the M.S. program at the university of this professor, and was working in the professor's research laboratory. It turned out that the student had been kicked out of the lab by the professor, and yet had still asked the professor to write a letter of recommendation. The professor obliged (for reasons that I cannot fathom) ... but was quite candid in the letter of "recommendation." Here are some excerpts from that letter:

"{Student X} was an average student...but because of {his/her} personality and personal problems {he/she} never lived to {his/her} potential. In the laboratory {Student X} never found {his/her} way. {He/she} frequently made foolish mistakes, and on two occasions caused fires in the lab. By the end of {his/her} second year, {he/she} had alienated {himself/herself} from the rest of my (research) group. In fact, my other group members were afraid of {Student X}. My group members informed me that {he/she} was often rude and hostile to them and other students. I regret that I cannot recommend {Student X} for your, or any other graduate program."

This is without a doubt the worst LOR that I have ever seen. Needless to say, we did not accept {Student X} into our program!
– Dr. Niles Lehman
Portland State University

GHOSTWRITING – GENERAL TIPS AND CONTENT OUTLINE

If one of your recommenders were to ask you to write or outline your own letter of recommendation, would you be prepared to do so? Be aware that this is a practical reality—it happens more commonly than you'd think. Perhaps you would feel that your recommender's request is inappropriate and unethical; if so, then do not pursue a letter from that recommender. If you decide to try ghostwriting the letter, however, you must take it very seriously.

It's one of the most ticklish tasks in the world—first, to try to write in the voice of your professor; second, to try praising yourself without going overboard or selling yourself short; and finally, to submit the draft to the professor for approval and hope they won't raise an eyebrow at either attempt. Needless to say, most college students have never written a letter of recommendation. When they sit down to rough out a first draft, they tend to freeze up as all sorts of new concerns arise: How long should the letter be? What should be included? What should be left out?

The following questions can serve as your guide to ghostwriting an effective and insightful letter of recommendation. Draft the letter of recommendation using these questions as your outline:

1. Who is the recommender? Include name, title, length of time at company/university, awards, etc.

2. How long has the recommender known the applicant?

3. Under what circumstances has the recommender known the applicant? Discuss projects, etc.

4. Does the letter include an anecdote of a specific experience that relates to the applicant's Core Themes?

I received two very similar (almost identical) letters within a week, from the same university in India. I wrote to both applicants, including copies of the letters, telling them that if they couldn't even bother to write their own letters, they shouldn't bother wasting my time. I received two very angry e-mails in response, whining about how it's alright for me sitting in an ivory tower in the USA, and how difficult it is for them in India. Needless to say both e-mails went straight into the wastebasket. Sadly, both CV's were of good quality, and they were probably ideal candidates, but their lack of imagination in something so simple as writing a letter was a big turn-off.
– Anonymous

5. If possible, explain how the applicant compares to other previous candidates for graduate school/employment. Compare applicant in terms of work performance and participation.

6. Does the letter include an assessment of the applicant's personality, character, and ethics?

7. In the opinion of the recommender, is graduate study or new employment appropriate at this time for the applicant? Why? Explain, citing specific examples to bolster the credibility of the application.

8. Does the letter include a strong statement of endorsement?

9. Does the letter include the recommender's signature?

Finally, we highly recommend that letters of recommendation be approximately two pages.

GHOSTWRITING: COMMON MISTAKES AND OMISSIONS

When a letter of recommendation fails to make an impression on the recipient, it's because it offers a description of the applicant that is too generic. The letter-writer either speaks in generalities that could apply to nearly any decent student, or neglects to include enough details about how well the applicant performs in relation to the crowd. Do your best to avoid these mistakes and omissions.

Once you have completed your draft of the LOR, ask yourself these questions about the letter:

1. Does the letter show how well the writer knows the applicant?

2. Does the letter show that the writer understands the applicant's professional/academic record and ability?

3. What does the writer say about the applicant's abilities and personal characteristics that are important for success in business school and after?

4. Does the letter explain the format in which the writer has seen the applicant perform? For example, has the applicant undertaken significant projects? Does the letter explain the type of interaction and involvement the applicant demonstrated with classmates or co-workers? How much contact did the writer have with the applicant outside work or the classroom?

5. Does the letter qualify the rigor the applicant has undertaken? The writer should clearly describe the level of difficulty of the work that the applicant has been involved with.

6. Is the applicant evaluated in the context of his or her peers? When possible, include a comparison of the applicant with other graduates or people from the same company who have gone on to business or graduate school. Such comparisons can give a more accurate assessment of the applicant's potential for success.

AVOIDING LOR LANGUAGE PITFALLS

A few years ago, two cultural anthropologists from Wayne State University conducted a groundbreaking study on academic letters of recommendation.[7] Frances Trix and Carolyn Psenka identified the microscopic ways in which ostensibly positive letters of recommendation can be sabotaged by the recommender's use of language. Their investigation focused on how semantic conventions tend to undervalue women's achievements, but we have seen inexperienced ghostwriters fall into many of the linguistic pitfalls they describe.

One of the expressed goals of Trix and Psenka's research was to help recommenders to edit their own letters for unintended signs of gender bias and omissions of essential topics. So we have turned their descriptive data into prescriptive action for ghostwriters. In other words, be alert for the unconscious tendency to describe your own gender in a stereotyped way, screen your draft for "doubt-raisers," and make a conscious effort to include more persuasive language if you discover that it's lacking.

---

7. "Exploring the Color of Glass: Letters of Recommendation for Female and Male Medical Faculty." Frances Trix and Carolyn Psenka. *Discourse & Society*, Vol. 14, No. 2, 191-220 (2003).

Description of general error	Prescription
Letter is too short	Make the letter longer (500 words is a good target) by including more detail.
Absence of LOR basic features (a.k.a. letter of minimal assurance)	Be sure the letter includes all of the following: INTRO: Commitment and relationship of evaluator to applicant BODY: Specificity of focus and record of applicant; Evaluation or comparison of academic traits and accomplishments of applicant Further detail of evidence of productivity in research, effectiveness in teaching, and collegiality in service, etc. CONCLUSION: A statement of recommendation

Description of doubt-raisers	Prescription
Apparent commendation (e.g., "Her performance was especially impressive, considering problems of which I have special knowledge.")	Tread carefully when discussing obstacles that were overcome by the applicant; the risk is that the letter will either provide "too much information" or appear patronizing (e.g., backhanded compliments).
Hedges (e.g., *seems to, tries to, apparently, looks to be*)	Cut the wishy-washy words.
Potentially negative comments	Be careful about using qualifying statements; in general, applicants are better described by what they are rather than what they are not.
Unexplained comments	Be wary of ambiguous statements that raise more questions than are answered.
Faint praise	The letter should praise actions or behavior that went above and beyond what was minimally expected.
Irrelevancies	Go easy on mentions of the applicant's personal life; avoid unprofessional references.
Inconsistency in naming practices	Be equitable in referring to applicants by full name or last name (vs. first name only).
Sex-linked descriptive terms	Examine each use of "lady," "female," "woman," etc. Are these terms truly necessary?
Inconsistent use of status terms or job titles	If the applicant has earned status terms or job titles, they should be mentioned.
Overreliance on grindstone adjectives (e.g., *hardworking, conscientious, dependable, meticulous, thorough, diligent, dedicated, careful*)	• These adjectives are not negative in themselves, but can take the place of more substantive comments about academic characteristics; for example, diligence can imply that the applicant must exert additional effort to compensate for lack of ability. • Solution: Put hard work in context.
Use of standout adjectives (e.g., *excellent, superb, outstanding, unique, exceptional, unparalleled*)	Consider repeating these words for emphasis.
Infrequent reference to high-status or high-value involvements, such as "research" or scientific terminology	• When describing research, try to cover all of the following: the applicant's particular project, aptitude in research design, and contribution to research environment. • Integrating scientific terminology or other "in-group" language can bulk up a LOR; a greater degree of detail suggests the recommender's interest in and support of the applicant's academic projects.
Imbalanced use of semantic realms following possessive pronouns (e.g., *his* career, *his* CV, *his* patients, *his* abilities/skills, *his* research, *his* colleagues vs. *her* students, *her* teaching, *her* personal life, *her* training)	• Take inventory of all words that immediately follow "his" or "her"—taken in total, do they portray the applicant as a researcher or a trainee, a (future) professional or a student? • Solution: Rewrite sentences to emphasize roles that you want to emphasize.
Overreliance on passive voice	Rewrite sentences into active voice to feature the applicant's agency.

TEMPLATE: GENERIC LETTER OF RECOMMENDATION
FOR A COLLEGE STUDENT, AS AUTHORED BY A PROFESSOR

To Whom It May Concern / Dear Sir or Madam:

It gives you[a] great satisfaction to recommend Applicant Surname for a position at Selective Institution or to support their application for Prestigious Program. You offer your judgment of Applicant Surname's suitability for the position based on your professional standing, stating your official job title and the length of time you have held it; if you like, you may elaborate by providing relevant details about your own educational background[b] and professional affiliations.[c] You are also qualified to discuss Applicant's candidacy based on your familiarity with his work. State how long you have known him and which course(s)[d] of yours he has enrolled in; also indicate the extent to which you observed and evaluated the quality of his character and the caliber of his academic performance. To round out this paragraph, it is common practice to provide a summarizing overview of Applicant's finest traits.[e] Finally, if you are planning to discuss any unusual or extenuating circumstances[f] relating to Mr. Surname's candidacy, you may want to alert the reader here; in general, however, because this is a letter of recommendation, the introductory paragraph should be limited to positive statements.[g]

If you have a charming anecdote about how Applicant Surname first came to your attention, such a story can easily launch a discussion of your interactions with Mr. Surname and the highlights of his academic record. Alternately, you may choose to begin by describing the course that Applicant enrolled in, briefly stating the learning objectives and/or grading structure[h] of the class. If Mr. Surname performed exceptionally in one or more of these areas, don't be shy about providing the details. Ideally, this is the section of the LOR where you provide several examples of his academic prowess or intellectual sophistication, for example, by lauding an ambitious thesis that was undertaken or research diligently conducted. Take a few lines to describe what he attempted, how well he succeeded, and why it impressed you. The more narrative specificity you provide about how Mr. Surname distinguished himself from the other students in the class, the more valuable your LOR is. If your impression of Applicant changed for the better during the course or subsequent acquaintance, devote a few lines to it; if you noticed substantial personal or intellectual growth, you would be doing Applicant Surname a serious disservice not to mention it in this letter.

Should you choose to discuss the grade that Mr. Surname earned in the class, do note for the record how many other students were enrolled in the course and what percentage of them earned the same grade. In addition to comparing Applicant to his immediate cohort, you may also choose to rank[i] him in comparison to all students who have ever taken that class, or all undergraduates you have ever worked with. When possible, rate Applicant Surname against past graduates who have been admitted to this particular Selective Institution or Prestigious Program; such a comparison can offer the Admissions Committee a more concrete context for your assessment of his potential for success. If you feel that Mr. Surname's performance was truly superlative, you might even pronounce him to be "in the top #" of students you have taught. [Ghostwriters, naturally, will not have access to these statistics; if you are drafting your own LOR, consider including a brief paragraph that addresses these class rankings, leaving the numbers blank. When your recommender reviews the LOR draft to make his or her revisions before signing the letter, they can choose to fill in the blanks at their discretion.] If Applicant Surname displayed precocious

a) Get directly to the point. You are under no obligation to provide a rhetorical or attention-grabbing preamble.
b) i.e., where you did your graduate or post-graduate training
c) e.g., credentials or membership in organizations or associations
d) State the grade he received, either here or in the second paragraph.
e) i.e., the ones you will be discussing in detail shortly; a simple list of adjectives will suffice.
f) e.g., potential concerns, or obstacles that he has overcome
g) It may sometimes be more efficient to draft and append these summarizing comments after you have actually written the body of the LOR.
h) e.g., how much emphasis was placed on attendance/participation vs. homework vs. quizzes/exams vs. term papers/projects
i) Use the percentages listed on the grid on the official LOR form, e.g., Upper 5%, Upper 10%, Upper Third, Middle Third, Lower Third.

critical thinking or writing, you can help the reader to visualize it by stating what grade level they were performing at relative to their age (e.g., *Although only a freshman, Applicant constructed essays that more resembled those of an upperclassman*, or *Mr. Surname's analysis showcased the complexity of argumentation that I expect from my graduate students*).

Mention any interaction you had with Applicant Surname outside of lecture. The detail of who initiated such contact is not insignificant, because readers of LORs[j] are generally interested in the applicant's interpersonal skills and the initiative he or she takes in seeking out mentorship or to help elucidate complex problems. A student's willingness to attend office hours is a good index of his motivation to utilize available resources to learn the material, to get past an impasse, or to seek informal career advising. If Applicant did consult you on any of these issues during your office hours, be sure to remark on Applicant's level of preparation, the quality of his questions, and his engagement with the material. If this interaction also offered you a window into his impetus for succeeding in the class, you may choose to extrapolate his larger motivations for choosing a particular career path.

Although not always feasible, one of the finest things you can do in a letter of recommendation is to situate Applicant Surname's academic accomplishments in a larger narrative about his passions, his competencies, and his career aspirations. From the other materials that Mr. Surname has provided to you—his transcript, his resume, his statement of purpose or personal statement—you may have gleaned certain thematic patterns that recur across his classroom achievements and his extracurricular activities. [k] Relate those themes to his desire to pursue higher academic study, and indicate how you believe Selective Institution or Prestigious Program fits into that narrative. Doing so serves two purposes: 1) it reinforces the themes that Applicant has chosen to emphasize in his application; 2) it further serves to humanize him, which will help him stand out from the competition.

Optional: At this point, you may decide to leaven your praise of Mr. Surname by mentioning one or two minor shortcomings, and how might these affect his ability to succeed at Selective Institution or Prestigious Program. Briefly identify a couple of areas where Applicant could stand to develop his skills or demonstrate growth. If he has already started to work on these weaknesses and made progress in overcoming them, this is all the more reason to mention it.

In some cases, this discussion may be linked to aspects of Mr. Surname's biography that involve social or educational obstacles. If you know of compelling reasons that the Admissions Committee should look beyond Mr. Surname's grade point average and standardized test scores in rendering their decision on his application, do not hesitate to draw these issues[l] to the Admissions Committee's attention. If possible, relate an anecdote here to illustrate how exceptional Applicant Surname's academic achievements truly are when situated in the context of challenges he has overcome, and obstacles that his peers did not have to face.

Conclude by summarizing the points made above and/or discussing Applicant Surname's potential to make a valuable contribution in his chosen field. You enthusiastically support Mr. Surname's candidacy because you believe strongly that his academic temperament and aspirations align well with the mission and high standards of Selective Institution or Prestigious Program. You express your confidence that he will not only thrive in that environment, but also add great vitality to the intellectual and social life of the program.

If you are willing to discuss Applicant Surname's qualifications in further detail, you make yourself available to the Admissions Committee by offering your contact number or email address.

Sincerely,

---

j) i.e., both graduate professional schools and potential employers

k) Especially activities involving leadership, service in the community, employment or internship experience.

l) Examples of relevant issues: if English was not Mr. Surname's first language; if he has handled unusual responsibility in his family; if he is the first in his family to attend college; if he was primarily responsible for financing his college education; if he carried a heavy load of extracurricular commitments.

TEMPLATE: GENERIC LETTER OF RECOMMENDATION
FOR AN EMPLOYEE, AS AUTHORED BY A MANAGER

To Whom It May Concern:

By way of introduction,[a] you identify your job title and the Company[b] that you work for, specifying your specific department and regional branch, if applicable. In a sentence or two, explain the range of your current professional responsibilities and the length of time you have been working for Company. You can conclude your self-introduction by citing prior work experience (duration and/or diversity) at other companies, to emphasize how familiar you are with the process of managing employees and evaluating their work performance.

You are writing to discuss Ms. Recommendee Surname's[c] work performance, as well as to offer your hearty endorsement of her professional skills. Indicate the duration and depth of your interaction with Ms. Surname; it commenced at Month Date, Year and continued to the present or Month, Year when she decided[d] to move on to new opportunities. During Ms. Recommendee Surname's tenure at Company, she was a valuable member of the firm, as you witnessed firsthand because you directly supervised her work. Finally, provide a quick laudatory overview of the personal and professional qualities you intend to elaborate upon in the next few paragraphs—the specific qualities the reader is seeking to confirm that Ms. Surname possesses.

You can start with your initial impressions of Ms. Surname and how she has lived up to or even exceeded those expectations as she integrated herself into the company culture. Describe how she earned your trust and confidence (e.g., *Because she consistently demonstrated an exceptional business sense and ability to grasp the big picture while never losing sight of the fundamentals, I came to rely on her implicitly*). If Ms. Surname was promoted from Initial Position to Current Job Title, don't forget to mention the part you played in approving or authorizing that promotion.

Alternately, you can leap straight into a discussion of her day-to-day responsibilities. You are not responsible for providing an exhaustive list of Ms. Surname's job duties.[e] Instead, you should describe her responsibilities from a manager's point of view; clarify which tasks she was initially assigned, and which responsibilities she asked for or earned the right to perform.

If you had to narrow down the qualities of Ms. Surname's to those you admire the most, they would be X, Y and Z. To illustrate X, you cite one particular instance that comes to mind: perhaps a project which Ms. Surname brought in on time and under budget, a client that she went out of her way to assist, or a series of presentations that she delivered to staff. Begin by sketching out the context and describing what was at stake: the outcomes that would depend on its successful execution, its importance to the department's operations or to the company's bottom line. Next, describe how Ms. Surname settled into her role; if she was immediately comfortable with the responsibility, that would suggest self-confidence and a proactive approach; if she took some time to inhabit the role fully, on the other hand, that could suggest growth. Don't forget to mention challenges or setbacks[f] as well as the attitude with which Ms. Surname addressed herself to resolving these issues. Emphasize her problem-solving ability. Be sure to remark on Ms. Surname's interpersonal skills; give examples of how she communicated her suggestions

---

a) These first two paragraphs can be easily reversed.

b) If your industry, products or services are relatively obscure, you may choose to devote a line to explaining Company's niche in the economy.

c) Your first mention of the recommendee should identify her by her full name and state the purpose of this letter.

d) If Ms. Surname's departure from Company was more complicated that this, you may want to save the details for later.

e) She will no doubt elaborate on them herself in her resume.

f) e.g., time pressures or limited resources

and needs with clarity, tact, and in a timely fashion. You might also comment on the integrity she showed by demonstrating a willingness to take responsibility for her commitments (and missteps).

If the results of her work (either on this particular project or in general) can be quantified in percentages or dollar amounts or man-hours, state it in these terms. To round out the anecdote, enlist the help of a chorus to help you sing the praises of Ms. Surname; discuss the feedback you received regarding her performance from management or clientele, as well as from the associates who worked with Ms. Surname. Link these traits to your observations on Ms. Surname's general sense of professionalism, however you define it. You would also do well to comment on Ms. Surname's relationship with management: her ability to accept constructive criticism from you or other higher-ups, the confidence or degree of trust Ms. Surname gained, etc. If you were responsible for writing her performance reviews, feel free to cite liberally from them. Rate her in comparison to other employees you have supervised and/or written letters of reference for.

At this point in the letter, you have several choices. You can: A) launch into another story, B) discuss Ms. Surname's weaknesses, or C) begin to wind down.

A: Every additional story[g] you tell should showcase another forte of Ms. Surname. If your first anecdote focused on Ms. Surname's grace under fire during a crisis, you might choose to balance it out with an example that illustrates her reliability and consistency over time.

B: If you feel obligated (or have been asked) to discuss Ms. Surname's professional weaknesses, point out traits that she could improve on. Presumably, since you have already brought up these issues with Ms. Surname during performance reviews, you will also be able to report on progress she has made towards addressing her weaknesses.

C: If you feel that a discussion of Ms. Surname's portfolio of "extracurricular" accomplishments is in order, mention your admiration for her commitment to a certain cause or activity. As always, you appear much more credible if you can support this assertion with a concise example of an act or practice she engaged in, including *who what where when why* details. If relevant, mention the time constraints or other pressures she had to work around in order to fulfill her commitments.

To conclude, you should neatly summarize how Ms. Surname was able to clearly set herself apart from her peers. If Ms. Surname demonstrates a certain set of traits that you find all too rare among employees at this stage in their career or otherwise displays exceptional ability, draw the reader's attention to it one last time. You reiterate that Ms. Surname makes the most of her natural talents, and cite the obvious effort she has devoted to developing new skills or building her knowledge base. You appreciate to the degree to which she is a well-rounded or multi-talented individual, exhibiting sets of traits that may not always go together in one person (e.g., she pairs technical skill with exceptional people skills, or praiseworthy productivity with a highly creative streak). You recap the excellent behaviors or practices that enables Ms. Surname to contribute substantially to the overall performance of the team. If relevant, wrap up by rating her potential for leadership. Drawing the letter to a close with the traditional flourish, your final sentence features a carefully chosen adjective ("Recommendee Surname would be an outstanding candidate for Stanford") and/or adverb ("I would strongly encourage you to hire Recommendee Surname for your team").

Kind regards,

---

g) Each one should include the same basic elements outlined above: 1 - Set the context; 2 - Describe how challenges were overcome; 3 - Appreciate the results.

SAMPLE LETTERS OF RECOMMENDATION

Adams High School

3546 Center Drive
Chicago, IL 34567

To Whom It May Concern:

It gives me immense pleasure to recommend Billy Apfelberg for admission to your university. He was my student in two classes last year, Algebra II/Trigonometry and Pre-Calculus, and in my five years of teaching at Adams High School, I count my experience with Billy as one of the most deeply satisfying stories of a student coming to discover self-motivation.

Fair or not, I had high expectations of Billy as soon as I saw his last name on the roster. I'd previously taught two of Billy's older brothers; both of them were extremely studious and had ranked among my highest-achieving students. Billy, the baby of the family, was more jocular, but not nearly as disciplined in his work ethic. He brought a sunny, generous personality; he was always eager to entertain his classmates. Even so, I sensed that he held a strong respect for the classroom. Although he sat with the unruly crowd, he loudly shushed them as soon as class started.

The grades I give are based on simple point accumulation. The total of 2000 points is divided as follows: 40% for eight tests, 40% for completing daily homework assignments, 10% for ten unannounced quizzes, and 10% for attendance.

On exams and quizzes, Billy consistently scored in the B to B+ range. As far as his daily homework habits, I couldn't help but notice that Billy consistently left the last few homework problems incomplete; he didn't even attempt to solve them. I knew it wasn't for lack of time, because most days I watched him do his homework. My prep period, when I grade tests and prepare lessons, immediately followed Algebra II/Trigonometry, happened to coincide with an empty class period for Billy. He asked permission to stay after class to complete his homework problems right away. After working out a friendly agreement that he would not engage me in idle chit-chat, I allowed him to use the classroom as his own private study hall.

It gave me the chance to ask him about his bad homework habit: why did he always stop a few questions short of completion? Billy admitted that while the word problems did perplex him occasionally, the main reason was a superstitious fear of doing his best. The only thing that surprised me about this admission was its frank self-assessment. I have seen this behavior before in other students; they have been told that they are B or C students, and to strive to get full points would betray an aspiration to truly succeed. I asked Billy to come up to the whiteboard. I told him his current point total (he was easily on track to get a B in the class) and I asked him whether it was mathematically possible—with 5 weeks left in the trimester—to get his point total up to 1800, which would allow me to give him a grade of A-. The answer was yes. According to our calculations, he needed to score an average of 95 on his remaining exams and quizzes—and turn in perfect homework. I reinforced this last point by asking him to calculate how many points he had lost already by turning in incomplete homework. When he realized that how much those niggling few points had already lowered his potential grade, it had exactly the desired effect.

Billy responded to the challenge. From that point on, he turned in complete homework, and every subsequent test held extra suspense for both of us, since he now had something at stake. And every time, we were thrilled. Realizing that he had lost points on previous exams due to careless mistakes, he began to ask me for extra exercises to practice.

I have no equivalent stories for Billy's performance in the class he subsequently took with me, because by the time he signed up for Pre-Calculus, he had clearly decided that he was an A student. His homework was impeccable, and his test scores reflected his new confidence. I even overheard him urging his classmates not to give up hope when they did badly on an exam. Watching a student come into his own power so dramatically—it pleases me beyond words. I feel very certain that Billy will bring this new academic maturity and ambition to your college, and share it with all the students that he comes into contact with. I recommend him wholeheartedly and with great enthusiasm.

If you have any questions that I can help clarify, please don't hesitate to contact me.

Sincerely,

North High School
257 Main St. San Francisco, CA 94010

To Whom It May Concern:

I write this recommendation for Janusz Karl with great pleasure. As his mentor for Radio Junior, a New Jersey Public Radio initiative that provides high school students in under-resourced neighborhoods with an intensive apprenticeship in professional radio journalism, I watched Janusz develop into a promising radio journalist in a short four months. He is an exceptionally charismatic young man with an infectious glee for "letting people know what their neighbors are doing." He will be an excellent addition to your university in general, and to the College of Journalism in particular.

As for my own credentials in the field, I have worked as an independent radio producer for the past five years; prior to that, I was responsible for developing new programs at WJUT. In the early 1990's I was co-creator and senior producer of "Pebblicious," an educational radio-drama series for children, for which I won the George Foster Peabody award.

During the first month of the Radio Junior workshop, Janusz was trained in the basics of news gathering and writing for radio broadcast. Along with 30 other teens, he learned everything from how to conduct an interview and develop a story to how to craft a script and digitally edit his audio.

The next two months were spent exploring various radio formats: news, commentary/monologue, and soundscape. Janusz's first story was on disability access issues at his high school. It was a fine example of straight news reporting that balanced multiple points of view. Next, he tried his hand at the personal essay, mixing a recollection of a trip to Panama with quirky musical bridges. It sounded for all the world like a segment from "This American Life" or "The Next Big Thing," which are, incidentally, two of his radio inspirations. For his soundscape assignment, Janusz mixed snippets of a family oral history tape with ambient groove music to produce a poignant tribute to his grandmother.

During the final month of the workshop, Radio Junior participants had free rein (and 20 hours of studio time) to make as many of their own radio items as they wanted, on the topics and in the format of their choice. Janusz went back to feature reporting, turning out pieces on a recent junk food ban at his high school, the controversy over vegan options at the cafeteria, and a playful primer to teenage slang.

He discovered that the decision to extend his three-minute radio segment by 30 seconds actually doubled the amount of research required to buttress the piece. He learned how to carefully expand the scope of the story without allowing it to swamp the focus. Actually, the first time it happened, he came to me and declared himself at an impasse. "Just tell me which subtopics to eliminate, please!" he pleaded, but I tossed the question back at him. As he listened to himself talk out the pros and cons of keeping each subtheme, the solution soon made itself clear, but more important, it was obvious that he had internalized the rules of feature writing. The point of this exercise was not lost on Janusz. From that point onwards, whenever he knocked on my door, he asked, grinning, "Is Mr. Sounding Board available?"

Upon completion of the workshop, Radio Junior participants work with the program directors to select one of their radio items to be aired on WJUT—usually during NPR's "Morning Edition." Janusz's piece on teen slang aired in April. Afterwards, when several people emailed to comment positively on the story, he was thrilled. So was I.

I have listened to Janusz's raw interviews as well as the finished news pieces, and I can testify that he gets great quotes because of the rapport that he establishes with his interviewees. He has an insouciant charm that encourages people to relax around him. At the same time, he doesn't coast on his native gifts. He throws himself into the research so that he can construct the smart questions that are most likely to elicit striking answers. He is excited about grounding himself in the structural underpinnings of effective radio journalism.

In terms of his personal radio presence, Janusz has honed his voice and timbre in debate club and in drama productions. He could be a professional speaker or an actor; actually, he has the physical presence to be an anchorman if he so chose. Fortunately for our profession, he seems intent on pursuing a lower-profile radio career, where he'll have to write his own copy and edit his own stories. Before too long, I fully expect to hear that Janusz Karl is covering the education beat on "All Things Considered" or making his own radio documentaries.

This was my first mentorship experience with Radio Junior, so I cannot offer a comparison of Janusz to other alumni of the program. However, as a producer for WJUT, I was responsible for supervising the college interns (11 in total), all of whom had college radio experience—and I would rate Janusz as their equal when it comes to diligence and potential. Do not hesitate to accept this young man into your program. He is talented, and in a few years time you will be proud to claim him as one of your distinguished alumni.

Sincerely,

Central Valley High School

To Whom It May Concern:

Samye Lhamo, is, in my opinion, one of the most promising scholar-athletes at Central Valley High School. I have coached her for the past three years on the junior varsity and varsity soccer teams, and based on my observations, she has what it takes to distinguish herself as a college athlete.

When she started high school, Samye had already been an all-star player in her youth league and her middle school intramural team, and was a veteran of several summer sports camps. During tryouts, I saw that she was strong, mobile, and loved to compete. She showed no fear at all. She clearly had great talent, but in our past experience, many precocious athletes who accept a Varsity position as freshmen end up sitting on the bench most of the year. I offered Samye a spot as a Varsity backup keeper, but I was honest with her about the amount of playing time she'd probably see. Her response? She asked me if she could play the majority of her games with JV as a starting midfielder but practice with the Varsity team—and get playing time in Varsity games against less competitive teams. I was impressed; she was showing me that she knew how important it was to keep herself sharp and in peak condition. I love to see that kind of drive in my athletes. I kept my promise by putting her on the field for Varsity games whenever I could; she worked hard and played aggressively every time. By the time we got to sectionals, a few injuries among our seniors gave me more flexibility with the Varsity lineup, and I was happy to move Samye up permanently to finish out the season. She was raring to go. Over the course of four postseason games, she had two assists and scored one of the winning goals to help the Wolverines advance to the CIF-SS Division I semi-finals. I knew she was good, but she literally got better with every game. Pressure brings out the best in her.

She started her sophomore season like a rocket. Graduating seniors had left a leadership vacuum on the field, but Samye stepped up and helped the Wolverines to post one of our best seasons in years. As I could have predicted, she was our leading scorer, scoring 11 goals and recording 7 assists against regular-season competition. She also continued to develop her defensive skills. Unfortunately, an injury limited her play towards the end of the season. Samye sustained a nasty shoulder sprain just before sectionals, which forced to withdraw for the rest of the season. Being named Pacific Western League MVP for regular-season play was gratifying, but couldn't quite compensate for the disappointment of missing the postseason. I know she wanted nothing more than to help lead her teammates in the playoffs.

She recovered in time to attend USC's summer soccer clinic, which had strict routines for physical conditioning. Samye came back from the experience with a renewed commitment to maintaining her fitness and conditioning; she started a weight-training regimen to get stronger for her junior year at Central Valley. This last season, Samye has had another excellent year, but what has really stood out for me is how she has matured as a leader. She looked first to distribute the ball to her teammates, and that approach worked. Her personal goals dipped slightly in the regular season to 10, but she led the team with 17 assists.

Samye has been listed on Central Valley High School's academic honor roll since her freshman year by maintaining a minimum GPA of 3.5. She was also one of ten student-athletes named to the league commissioner's list, honoring distinguished players who achieved a grade point average of 3.75 or higher last year. Somehow she manages a full course load while training year round and holding down a part-time job. Her time management skills must be superb.

Samye Lhamo is a gracious competitor, a committed team player, and approaches all challenges with easy self-confidence. Her thirst to constantly improve her skills is unquenchable. Every coach loves having a player of that caliber on his team. I have no doubt that she will be a valuable asset to your athletic program.

Sincerely,

To Whom It May Concern:

I am delighted to write on behalf of Mabel Zhang, and in support of her application for the medical program at your university. I have taught in the History Department at the University of East Great Falls for five years, and at the University of Colorado for the ten years prior. During that time, I have recommended more than 200 students for graduate study; approximately ten of those students were asking me to support their application to medical school. Of that group, I would easily categorize Mabel Zhang as the one with the most potential to succeed.

Ms. Zhang earned an A last year in my course, History 198: The Social Context of Medicine. The class enrollment was approximately 200, and the grading was based on a midterm exam, an oral presentation, and a final exam. I actually met Ms. Zhang on the first day of class, when she petitioned to enroll in the upper-division class as a sophomore. I hesitated at first, warning her that the class would require a level of academic rigor that she might not be ready for, but she explained that she was a Biology and Gender Studies double major, and that she would not have time in her schedule over the next two years to take this course (one of the few which satisfies the Gender Studies disciplinary breadth requirements) before she graduated. With a final admonition that she should be proactive about seeking help, I approved her petition—and she took my words more seriously than I could have imagined.

Ms. Zhang became a regular presence at my office hours; each time, she came prepared with a list of questions about the lecture I had just given. Her passion for the subject was ferocious, and her questions suggested a level of intellectual curiosity and critical thinking that I am more accustomed to seeing in my graduate students. Unlike most of the other science majors who find their way into my classes, Mabel approached the readings and the writing assignments with real delight.

Each student was expected to present an oral report on the history of a particular disease or epidemic; most focused their presentation on disease etiology, symptoms and relevant therapies, Mabel chose tuberculosis because she wanted to discuss not only sex-based difference but also gender differences in the incidence, diagnosis and treatment of a disease. She also—with my permission—included video footage in an irreverent yet incisive presentation that left the entire class in stitches.

As it turns out, her investigation of the influence of gender (in conjunction with but differentiated from sex difference) in pathology proved to be a fruitful line of research for her. Mabel asked so many questions about this topic that I encouraged her to pursue the answers by writing a research paper at some future point; when she asked if such an assignment could substitute for this class's midterm exam, I agreed.

I was impressed with the final paper's ambition and execution. Mabel drew a convincing analogy between historical and contemporary perceptions of migraine as a hysterical "women's disease," and was able to marshal fascinating primary sources to support her thesis. In the end, the scope was a little too big for a 15-page paper, which prompted me to assign it a grade of A-, but I encouraged her to develop the ideas further in a longer paper. I understand that she is currently expanding the paper into an honors thesis. She had asked me to serve as her independent study advisor, and I would have liked nothing more than to continue to nurture this rare intellect, but I had to decline; I would be leaving for a fellowship year in France and therefore unable to supervise her research properly. However, I referred Ms. Zhang to a colleague in the History department, who assures me that the thesis is taking shape beautifully. Mabel has promised to share the paper with me as soon as she finishes it this spring.

Mabel Zhang is a humane scientist who will succeed in any field she chooses. She had confided to me that she was drawn to both medicine and to further study in the liberal arts. I would not hesitate to recommend her for graduate study in History, but now that she has decided to make her career in medicine, I can only say that her future teachers, classmates and patients will be much the richer for it. She will be the kind of physician who understands the medical humanities in her marrow.

I feel honored to have played a part in Mabel Zhang's intellectual development, and I urge you to accept her into your medical program.

Sincerely,

Fairmont University

To Whom It May Concern:

I am the head of Chemistry at Fairmont University with a joint appointment in the Department of Earth and Ocean Sciences. My research focuses on the isolation and structure elucidation of novel organic metabolites produced by marine organisms.

I am truly enthused about recommending Marc Bellingham for medical studies. For nearly a year, I have had the great pleasure of supervising Marc Bellingham's work in my laboratory. He took the position of student intern in my laboratory in order to gain research experience in natural-product chemistry, and over the past ten months, he has made many valuable contributions to our laboratory.

Marc has been impressive with his independent work as well as his ability to integrate himself into our interdisciplinary research team. A few days after joining our lab, I asked him to give a presentation to some of our collaborating colleagues in the chemistry department about bioprospecting and the properties of Flabellina gracilis, the aeolid nudibranch that our lab has been studying. He did an excellent job researching the materials, preparing the PowerPoint slides, and giving an informative presentation on intervertebral biology and ethical bioharvesting to our chemistry colleagues. Marc has become an integral member of our biochemistry studies team, playing a vital role from the beginning of a study to its conclusion. Some of our studies focus on defensive metabolites found in the skin extracts of nudibranchs, and I have assigned Marc to assist the researchers in my lab who are focused on using stable isotope methodology to study the de novo biosynthesis of terpenoid and polyketide metabolites. Marc helps prepare the F. gracilis specimens by feeding the nudibranches their appropriate precursors, on a regimented daily schedule, via syringe injection through their dorsum into the hepatopancreas. He is also responsible for generating and harvesting skin extracts by immersing the nudibranches in methanol, and partitioning the specimens by solubility in various reagents for the different research projects. Lastly, he analyzes the fractionation of the ethyl acetate-soluble materials in preparation for loading into the chromatography fixtures.

Marc regularly works alongside our chemistry expert, Dr. Harold Korvasian, and my visiting scholar, oceanographer Dr. Alice Sung. Marc has helped to streamline many of our lab protocols by conducting background literature reviews and actively involves himself in the planning and discussion meetings with Drs. Korvasian and Sung. He has shown initiative by studying biochemistry and marine biology texts in order to understand his lab assignments and to be more effective in his work. I believe Marc's ability to work efficiently and independently arises from his aptitude and enthusiasm for new challenges, which will serve him well in his future career.

From the start, Marc showed his eagerness for learning by carefully observing Dr. Korvasian perform the spectroscopic analysis of the metabolites. After Dr. Korvasian remarked to me about how he could often trust Marc to run our sophisticated testing protocols on his own, Marc was approved to autonomously operate the silica gel flash chromatographer as well as to run the reversed-phase high pressure liquid chromatography machine. Often, individual studies will require different testing protocols, which Marc has shown himself capable of programming into the HPLC computer terminal. His attention to detail and careful observations have also helped improve the reliability of our data by his analysis of when a test needs to be repeated or reassessed.

Subsequent to the actual testing, Marc is involved in the data analysis work such as data formatting, statistical analysis, and the actual figure preparations for the manuscript. It is crucial that the tests be done in a timely manner to prevent biological degradation of the metabolites from affecting the results, and Marc has shown his dedication by taking the data analysis work home with him, as well as coming in on weekends to conduct feeding or run tests.

We have found Marc to be an excellent writer. In some of our latest studies, he has been co-authoring as well as independently authoring sections of the manuscript. In fact, he has taken on a larger role with each subsequent study we do. He has even been entrusted with second author responsibilities for some of our latest studies with terpenoid and polyalkaloid biosynthesis, which will also be submitted to the Journal of Natural Products.

In terms of character, I have found Marc to be very personable and helpful. When Dr. Alice Sung first arrived last fall, Marc was kind enough to show Dr. Sung around the university and help her acclimate to her new work environment and surroundings. Two of our visiting scholars are from China, and do not speak English as a first language. Marc has been very helpful in giving his time to assist them with tasks requiring the use of English. Regardless of whether the task involves the formalized language of a scientific paper or common colloquialisms and idioms, Marc does not hesitate to tutor or explain when asked.

Marc has very wisely used his time after graduation to gain exposure to the medical profession as a clinical volunteer at the university hospital. I am also very impressed with Marc's community contributions and involvement. His leadership with the Flying Samaritans and mentoring role as peer counselor are representative of his interpersonal skills and aptitude for working with diverse individuals.

As far as commenting on his readiness for the rigors of medical school, I would like to point out that Marc's academic aptitude is amply documented. He graduated with honors and with distinction, and his GPA (overall 3.84; science 3.87) helped to earn him a Phi Beta Kappa nomination in his junior year. Accomplishing all this at Fairmont University amidst the high competition among undergraduate pre-meds places him among a higher echelon of candidates. In addition to his work in my lab, Marc's capacity and enthusiasm for research is also exemplified by the breadth of his research background in organic chemistry and medical legislation issues.

I believe Marc can contribute to a vibrant medical student community with his multiple talents and skills. In terms of comparing him to other pre-med students I have worked with, I would evaluate him as being in the top 5%. Based on our many meetings and discussions, and a thorough perusal of his personal statement, I feel comfortable recommending Marc Bellingham as a mature candidate for medical school.

Sincerely,

Cross Lutheran Bread of Healing Clinic

To Whom It May Concern:

As the coordinator of the HIV Prevention Project for the Cross Lutheran Bread of Healing Clinic, I have had the great pleasure of working with Petra Czehelszky, who has been one of our most dedicated and valuable employees for the past year and half. She is one of three Clinic Assistants who help me run the program, and the clinic is very fortunate to have somebody of her skills and talents. I am consistently impressed with her maturity and professionalism. I fully support her desire to become a physician, and her decision to pursue osteopathic medicine.

The Bread of Healing Clinic is a free medical clinic that serves the uninsured and underinsured. Our HIV Prevention Project works with persons infected and affected by HIV/AIDS by providing support services and works to prevent HIV infection through information and education. On a daily basis, Petra's duties involve counseling and providing case management services for newly-diagnosed HIV+ individuals and other low-income clients who cannot obtain medical care. The large and diverse population includes many injection drug users who are often dealing with some combination of the difficult issues of street living, poverty, and physical and mental health problems. The site where Petra and I work together is in the North side neighborhood, which is a very poor and isolated community; many of our clients there have little reason to trust anyone.

Petra has demonstrated a wonderful ability to connect with the different individuals using our service. First of all, she is very punctual and dependable, because she recognizes the importance of consistency for the clients. She is very non-judgmental, personable, genuinely interested in people's well-being, and can make strangers feel comfortable immediately. Her great listening and communication skills help her handle conflicts with clients thoughtfully and calmly. When patients lash out or snipe, Petra never takes it personally – she holds them in a compassionate gaze until they are ready to have a dialogue again. She remarked to me once, after a patient spit on her, "He's in so much pain right now."

In a way, it doesn't seem fair to compare the average 21-year-old pre-med applicant with a non-traditional applicant like Petra. Younger students can be precociously mature; a woman like Petra emanates a deep equanimity that has been tested and tempered over years. I think this has everything to do with her background as a domestic relations mediator, and her training in Non-Violent Communication (NVC) principles. Early on, Petra explained NVC to me as a language technique that teaches people to observe actions in a non-judgmental way, to identify the feelings and needs that come up, and then to request that these needs be fulfilled. She suggested that the clinic staff might benefit from learning more. I agreed, and asked her to organize an in-service where a certified NVC trainer could teach us the basics. Many of us—myself included—had been operating intuitively by those principles, but to hear them formally articulated was a bit of a revelation. We've all benefited from the experience.

I also want to note that my use of the word "equanimity" is not a euphemism for "staid" or "humorless." Petra's laugh is a delighted cackle – it's warm, unmistakable and infectious. We hear it several times a day, and I think it's another reason why Petra's clients trust her immediately and want to talk to her.

I predict that when Petra starts medical school, her younger classmates will automatically defer to her; and she will be gracious about taking on leadership roles when others insist, but she will also redistribute the authority so that everybody feels deeply engaged and involved. I have seen it happen here at the clinic. When new volunteers arrive, they quickly begin following Petra around as if she were a mother duck. In a week or two, however, she has helped give them the training and confidence to act decisively on their own; they begin to see themselves as empowered. Imagine how useful this skill will be in educating patients. From what I know about osteopathic medicine, I believe this behavior is very much in line with that philosophy as well.

Whenever I write recommendations for individuals, I always try to highlight some kind of growth, because I know that the schools and future employers who read these letters are keenly interested in the applicant's potential to assimilate the training they'll be given and re-express it in the form of developed knowledge and competent technique. But Petra came to the clinic having already mastered those. Her seasoned experience gives her the ability to look at each person's individual needs and quickly assess what she can do to help, whether it be simply listening with compassion, offering a little information, or initiating a serious discussion that will include handling difficult questions. She is scrupulously accurate with the information she provides. If she is not able to help someone directly, she will find out where to refer them and make sure they have the proper contacts. She remembers all of her clients by name and follows up later by asking them about their situation.

She is such a consistently mature and thoroughly reliable presence that I occasionally forget that she is only a clinic assistant. I tend to think of her as a colleague – she simply inspires that kind of trust. I wish I had ten Petras working for me. I wish that clinics across the country all had somebody like her.

And so I offer Petra my highest recommendation. I only regret that the clinic will lose her services, but I know that she is serious about serving the community. When she returns, it will be as the marvelous physician that she is so clearly destined to be. If you would like to contact me with any questions, please feel free to do so.

Sincerely,

West Dearborn Ambulance Corps
12 Centre Dr. Meyer, NY 10379

To Whom It May Concern:

Frederika Giouzelis has my staunch support for her medical school application. I have worked for 11 years as an EMT-Paramedic for the West Dearborn Ambulance Corps. We are a Municipal Third Service that operates alongside fire and police departments. Over the past nine months, Frederika Giouzelis has worked a double shift nearly every weekend as an EMT-Basic for my ambulance crew. During that time, she has routinely performed basic cardiac life support (CPR), basic and advanced airway maneuvers, oxygen therapy, extrication, splinting, IV preparation and a number of other procedures; she is also proficient at operating a semi-automatic defibrillator. "Freddie," as she is known to the team, has matured into a seasoned, capable field medic. She is a valued member of my team.

She earned her EMT license after passing a driving program, and being tested on EMS Standard Operating Procedures, patient care protocols, proper radio techniques and incident command. Before working on my team, Freddie spent a month on a Basic Life Support (BLS) ambulance crew, which mostly did non-emergency medically supervised transportation of patients being transferred between hospitals and nursing homes. Then she put in a request to be transferred to an Advanced Life Support crew because it would give her more exposure to medically significant emergencies and techniques (e.g., transcutaneous pacing, synchronized cardioversion and intubation).

Although nobody would ever describe our job as lighthearted, I do recall Freddie's first shift as being unusually difficult. In the space of one weekend, we were called to the scene of two teen suicides, a grisly multiple-car pileup, and three young children who had been killed by their father. In a couple of these cases, there were a few victims who still showed a heartbeat when we arrived on scene, but our reviving measures just didn't work. Time after time, there was simply nothing we could do for the people we were supposed to help. In some ways it was the worst possible introduction to the job of an EMT-Paramedic; in other ways, it was a bracing lesson in the reality of how grim our work can be at times. Freddie took it hard; she began to talk about returning to the BLS crew, or at least taking some time off. I took her aside and reminded her that she could speak to a counselor for a Critical Incident Stress Debriefing; I also told her that in my opinion, the best way to get past this was to get back to work. Feeling helpless, unfortunately, is something that does happen occasionally in our line of work; but if the cure for grief is action, then we EMTs are in the best possible position to heal ourselves.

Freddie bounced back. Since that first rough patch, she has been personally responsible for reviving and stabilizing several patients, which is a very affirming, confidence-building experience. But I think it's the eight months of practical experience, punching in week in and week out, that has helped her truly internalize the message I tried to convey early on: that we can't let the emotions from one incident get in the way of handling the next call. Just last week, a new EMT trainee did a couple of ridealongs with us. I asked Freddie to brief him on the realities of our job. She told him: "Most of the time we get to use our skills to make a real difference. Sometimes we fail. That's not a reason not to keep going."

Freddie tells me that she would eventually like to work in the trauma surgery center of an urban hospital. Like all of us, she clearly thrives on the adrenaline and the feeling that she can bring control and order to a situation that's very chaotic. However, she never lets that heightened sense detract from her ability to remember that we are dealing with real people and their emotions. Two incidents in particular come to mind. A teenage boy had committed suicide by hanging himself in his garage. We arrived, and Freddie was helping me cut him down. In the commotion, nobody noticed that the victim's younger sister, who knew nothing of the incident, had just come home from school. Freddie was the one who saw the girl walking up the driveway. She quickly moved to block the view of the garage before leading the child to her parents. The alertness Freddie showed spared the girl additional trauma; that kind of quick-thinking sensitivity comes instinctively to her, as I have witnessed repeatedly.

Freddie's language skills also make her an especially useful first responder. Her ability to communicate in both Farsi and Arabic has been invaluable to us, since our service area includes neighborhoods with a high concentration of immigrants from the Middle East. I remember one scene with the distraught mother of a young boy who had been hit by a car in the road. They managed to stabilize him in the ER, but when he subsequently lapsed into a coma, we then had the grim task of telling his mother that her child might not wake up. Freddie handled the situation with extreme sensitivity. The mother told us afterwards she was deeply grateful to have had somebody there who could explain her son's medical situation to her in her own language.

I have had the privilege of watching Freddie develop into a deeply competent EMT. Far from being discouraged by witnessing situations where medicine cannot bring people back to life—she is motivated to strive even harder when it can. When she believes a patient can be saved, she will exhaust herself to fan the spark back into a flame; more than once, this unflagging effort of hers has made the difference. The medical profession needs more such dedicated practitioners. Based on my evaluation of Freddie Giouzelis' performance as an EMT, I believe she is eminently prepared at this time to further her medical training.

Sincerely,

NEBRASKA STATE UNIVERSITY

To Whom It May Concern:

It is not often that I completely rewrite a letter of reference for a pre-medical applicant, but I am pleased to make the exception for Veronica Balignasay. I am the Health Professions Advisor at Nebraska State University. Last year I wrote a letter recommending Veronica Balignasay as an applicant for several osteopathic medical schools. She seemed very bright and eager, but I could not give my strongest endorsement because my acquaintance with her was so brief; moreover, her patient contact experience and exposure to osteopathic medicine were relatively slight; for example, she had shadowed an osteopathic physician, Dr. Valerie Eastman, on a single occasion.

In comparison to the total number of pre-meds that I encounter in any given year who are intent on pursuing a career in osteopathic medicine, Ms. Balignasay's qualifications placed her in the top 20% or so; as an undergraduate pre-medical student, she was "merely" above-average. However, she has pursued the reapplicant's path with a fervor that I have rarely encountered in others in her situation. First, she diligently sought out feedback from medical schools about their reasons for denial—and enlisted my help on one or two occasions to dig deeper; then she treated their suggestions for improvement—as well as my own—as a serious personal assignment. Over the past twelve months, she has taken clear, concrete steps to substantially upgrade her academic and non-academic credentials.

Consequently, I am submitting a new letter on Veronica's behalf because her candidacy has improved, in my opinion, to the point where she seems almost to be a new candidate. I can now say with assurance that the promise she showed a year ago has manifested itself clearly in all of the following areas: academics, research, community service and clinical experience. To tackle improvements in so many areas in a relatively short period of a year is no small task; I believe that the effort exerted—and the accomplishments produced—are a testament to Veronica's resilience and tireless dedication to her goals. To wit:

Academics: To demonstrate that the lowest grades on her transcript are not reflective of her true abilities and motivation, Veronica retook the second semester of O-Chem at a junior college, raising her grade from C- to a solid B.

Research: Shortly after graduation, Veronica landed a part-time internship assisting a clinical study survey coordinator. Five months ago, she made the transition into a full-time position, Assistant Clinical Data Coordinator. On a daily basis, she helps maintain operations of various Phase II clinical trials involving aneurysm patients by visiting sites to monitor the logistical distribution of forms, laboratory samples and supplies, and to ensure site compliance with protocol specifications, FDA, and other regulatory obligations.

Volunteer Work: She has made a unique service contribution to the community by sharing her passion for yoga with a local women's shelter. On her own initiative, Veronica approached the director of the Monte Rosa Safe Home and volunteered to lead weekly yoga classes for the domestic violence survivors as part of their healing process. I admire the creativity with which she integrated her avid interest in holistic health with her desire to serve the less fortunate. From all reports, the classes have been very well-received by the clients of the women's shelter; in fact, the demand is so great that Veronica has been looking for ways to expand the program.

Clinical Experience: Over the past year, she has pursued meaningful and substantial exposure to osteopathic medical practice by continuing to shadow Dr. Eastman for one day each month. Two months ago, she also supplemented her clinical experience when she began working four (4) hours a week at the triage desk for a local Emergency Room.

Without question, Veronica's overall pre-medical profile has become both broader and deeper. I believe that you will find she has very conscientiously applied herself to targeting all the areas in which her pre-med preparation could be considered underdeveloped and reinforcing them with solid achievement. Veronica has assured me that she intends to forge ahead with her new commitments up until the day she matriculates into medical school; In other words, if you like the Veronica Balignasay you see now—and I frankly think you should—you'll love the Veronica Balignasay who shows up on the first day of class. When I talk to her now, I am impressed by the exceptional focus with which she speaks about the osteopathic practice that she envisions for herself. She is committed to growing her technical knowledge, her research skills, and her community connections.

Sincerely,

Joseph Cottrell, M.D.
17 Manchester Rd. Boston, MA 55555
(555) 555-1112

To Whom It May Concern:

 This is the tale of a pharmacy school hopeful who must beat the odds of a sub-par GPA and test scores. It's an underdog story and the American dream all rolled into one, and I'm proud to have the chance to tell it. The hero of the story is Seng Moua, a Hmong refugee who prefers to be called by his American name, Craig.

 My name is Joseph Cottrell, and I am the president of the Toastmasters chapter where Craig has blossomed into an excellent communicator and leader over the past two years. I am also a practicing physician (Dartmouth Medical School, Class of '78), and I strongly advocate Craig Moua's candidacy for pharmacy school

 I cannot know if any of Craig's other recommenders will address this issue, so I will state it in no uncertain terms: Craig's undergraduate grades do not reflect his current verbal ability or his communication skills. And If your school is one that considers an applicant's PCAT score to be an integral part of the application, I would say to you: please consider the whole candidate.

 Craig's undergraduate grade point average was sandbagged by one academic subject: English. His PCAT score was hobbled by his performance on the Reading Comprehension section. Both can be explained in large part by Craig's ESL history. When Craig came to the States as a 14-year-old, after living in a refugee camp near Bangkok for more than a decade, he knew no English. Therefore, in the past eight years or so, he has progressed from the ABC's and ESL classes to applying for graduate studies in his second language. The fact that immigrants do this all the time does not make it any less extraordinary.

 I know about Craig's history because he told it to us in the very first speech that he gave as a Toastmasters member. It was an "Icebreaker" speech, one designed to ease a novice speaker's nerves and give them the chance to introduce themselves. Craig spoke, as one might expect, about the refugee camp where he'd spent so much of his life; quite unexpectedly, however, he chose to focus most of the speech on his silliest memories. His delivery was still rough around the edges, but we the audience found ourselves laughing and wiping at our eyes. Not many people can inspire both chuckles and tears with their very first speech; I knew Craig was worth keeping an eye on. Then, for his second speech, he spoke very earnestly about why he wanted to be a pharmacist. As an M.D., I took a special interest in Craig's situation. I felt that I was in a position to offer this budding young pharmacist my personal and professional support.

 I offered to be Craig's Toastmasters mentor, and I was gratified to see how hard he worked to improve himself. He rehearsed like mad, but also learned to relax and accept the constructive criticism that comes with the peer evaluation of every performance. Craig even asked me for special coaching on reducing his accent.

 He worked his way through the 10-speech manual that led to his designation as a Competent Communicator. Not content to stop there, Craig is now already halfway through the Success/Leadership series. From the start, it was clear that he loved combining his passions for communicating and for pharmacology; many of his speeches have dealt with pharmaceutical medicine and physiology in some form or another. For example, in the "Show What You Mean" speech that challenges Toastmasters to make effective use of gesture and body language, he gave a five-minute anatomy lesson; he donned a large white plastic trash bag (with cutouts for head and arms) and then drew organ systems on it with a marker. For the "Be Persuasive" speech, Craig tackled the controversial issue of drug re-importation. For the "Speak With Knowledge" speech, he tackled the latest news in antibiotic resistant bacteria. Whenever he speaks about his intellectual love, he just lights up. His speeches are beautifully organized. His analogies are funny and very apt. His audience is entertained even as it is being educated.

If Craig hadn't already wanted to pursue a career in academic pharmacy, all this would have prompted me to urge him to consider a teaching career. Given his talents, I have no doubts at all that the future Professor Moua will quickly win a loyal following among his students. On a related note, he has learned to give incisive evaluations of his fellow Toastmasters. He is tactful but his advice is always spot-on. People look forward to receiving his comments.

It's unfortunate that Craig did not discover Toastmasters earlier. I truly believe that if he had joined our group before his senior year of college, the amazing growth that I've seen in Craig as a communicator—both in terms of confidence and technique—would have translated into better grades in his lower-division composition classes. Let me say a bit more about that now. As a freshman and sophomore, the transcript indicates, Craig earned solid C's and C-minus's in various composition and literature classes. Most individuals who had only been living in an English-language environment for five years (at that time) might consider average grades quite an accomplishment. Craig knew, however, that it would be perceived as a problem in his application and was therefore an obstacle to his goals. His science GPA was 3.4, but his overall GPA was 2.8. He took substantial action to improve himself in this regard, and the effort paid off in his upper-division writing class (grade: B). Since graduating a year ago, he has enrolled in an extra class or two (Contemporary Fiction, grade: B+; Technical Writing, grade: A-) to demonstrate that he is capable of successfully keeping up with a reading load and writing requirements. He's clearly grown in his abilities.

Consider this as well: When he gives his evaluations of his fellow speakers, Craig Moua can recite back entire passages of their speeches without looking at his notes. I mention this not simply to suggest that he has a rare talent for listening (won't his patients love that!) but to suggest to you that visual processing of texts (i.e. reading) is not his preferred mode of assimilating new information. Pharmacy school will require him to memorize formulae and reactions in spades, of course, but each student also takes responsibility for figuring out how he can learn that information most efficiently; Craig is already cultivating alternative study habits, as you can infer from his academic success in the recent writing classes.

For most immigrants, immersion in a foreign culture and language is somewhat of a necessary evil – a scalding hot bath that one tests with one's toes – grudgingly, fearfully. By joining Toastmasters, Craig plunged in boldly. To stand up in front of strangers and hold forth in a language you know yourself to be shaky in – that either takes incredible courage or indomitable drive. In Craig Moua's case, I would say it was both. He will bring great passion and commitment to his pharmacy studies. I want to see him succeed. I strongly recommend that you give him the opportunity to do so.

If you require further information, please do not hesitate to contact me.

Sincerely,

Mountain View
Riding Center

434 Lake Road
Albuquerque, NM 55555

To Whom It May Concern:

It gives me great pleasure to support Sujit Kumarasinghe's application for the Master's program in Physical Therapy. I am the Therapeutic Riding Program Director of the Mountain View Riding Center. For the past six months, I have supervised Sujit in his role as a hippotherapy volunteer at our center. I signed off on every one of his 110 hours of service, so I can testify to the zeal with which he devoted himself to learning about this unique mode of physical rehabilitation, as well as to participate in patient care. In my opinion, he certainly has the potential to complete the graduate program as well as a personal compatibility with physical therapy as a profession. I find Sujit's ability to quickly establish rapport with patients striking; I think it has to do with his humane sense of purpose, his quick thinking, and his sincere desire to make other people as comfortable as possible. He has demonstrated great compassion for patients and an avid interest in educating himself about alternate physical therapeutic treatment modalities.

To briefly state my qualifications for evaluating Sujit: I received my Doctor of Physical Therapy degree from the University of Cincinnati, and I have 20 years of experience as a physical therapist; I am also a certified riding instructor with the North American Riding for the Handicapped Association (NARHA), a longtime member of both the United States Equestrian Federation and United States Dressage Federation. I helped establish the Hippotherapy Program at Mountainview more than ten years ago when the science began to support what I had informally observed myself for many years: that the motion of a walking horse positively stimulates the rider, and can help enhance balance, posture, mobility, coordination and strength in individuals diagnosed with a wide variety of neurological, skeletal, muscular and emotional disorders.

In order to become a certified hippotherapy volunteer, Sujit went through our training program. This means that he understood the aforementioned treatment principles and proved competence in equine skills. Because of his premedical and kinesiology studies, the former came very easily for him; as for his experience with horses, he began as a relative novice, but he quickly acquired basic handling, grooming, tack fitting and leading skills, along with rudimentary horsemanship. It soon became clear that he had fallen in love with all of his four-legged co-workers. More than once, Sujit told me how fortunate he felt to be able to combine his interest in health care with the chance to work with such magnificent creatures.

Out in the yard, Sujit was qualified to serve as one of the side walkers who flank either side of the horse for added safety when patients undergo their riding therapy. His duties as a volunteer also involved helping to register new patients, to help orient them to the center, and to give tours of the stables to prospective patients. In all of these interactions, Sujit was consistently friendly, helpful and professional.

In order to illustrate the outstanding traits that I have observed in Sujit, I would like to tell you a story about a patient that he formed a special connection with. Breanna Louie is an 8-year-old girl who suffers from ataxic cerebral palsy. When Breanna's mother brought her in for the first riding appointment, the girl was very eager to get started. However, as soon as we introduced her to Jumble, the horse she would be riding, she began to cower and cry. She was clearly frightened by the size of a real horse.

Sujit saw this, and led her back into the waiting room, where he produced a toy horse to distract her. "Do you think you could sit on this horse?" he asked. He found a doll and they began to roleplay the type of riding she would be doing. I watched him emphasize that Jumble would not be galloping but instead walking at a slow, measured pace. Then he offered to take her on a tour of the stables; he held her hand the entire time. This calmed Breanna down considerably, and after about 10 minutes she declared that she was ready to get on "the jumbo horse."

Breanna wanted Sujit to ride behind her on Jumble. However, the role of back rider (the individual who supports patients who are not able to sit unassisted on the horse) is reserved for licensed physical or occupational therapists, so we could not permit him to ride with her. Sujit told Breanna, though, that he was thrilled to be one of the side walkers and that he would stay very close to her. He helped her put on her helmet. The hippotherapist who was riding with Breanna saw that the girl had bonded with Sujit and obligingly slipped into a low-key role. Breanna addressed all her comments to Sujit, and he responded encouragingly. It was good to hear her giggles.

As soon as Breanna and her mother left, Sujit apologized to us for monopolizing the girl's attention. With his humility, it was clear that he felt embarrassed for having "upstaged" the professional therapist. We assured him there was nothing to apologize for. Our goal is for our patients to enjoy the riding experience; Breanna had clearly formed a trusting bond with him that was integral to her enjoyment—and help make the therapy an activity that they will look forward to. Besides that, I find that we are so used to thinking of problem-solving as a rational, cognitive act that we sometimes forget that authentic needs-assessment and loving communication also have their place in helping people moving past an impasse.

On all her subsequent visits, Breanna asked for Sujit as soon as she arrived. Once or twice he had to rearrange his work schedule in order to be there for her; we did not ask him specifically to do this; rather, he understood the responsibility that came with the relationship.

He also took the initiative to study up on cerebral palsy—and Breanna's type in particular—to more fully understand how the horseback riding was helping to improve her muscle tone, motor control and sense of balance. I can assure you that she is not the only patient whose medical condition he has striven to learn more about. Sujit regularly asked the riding center's resident therapists about the nuances of the pathophysiological symptoms presented by the hippotherapy patient, as well as our respective training and practice; we were happy to answer his questions when we could, and to refer him to other colleagues or resources when his avid curiosity went beyond our personal areas of expertise.

To sum up, Sujit helped our staff provide an excellent level of care and demonstrated a remarkable ability to form easy, productive relationships with patients. It thrilled him to watch patients make progress with their mobility, strength, and attitude. I have supervised many aspiring physical therapy students over the years and Mr. Kumarasinghe is easily among the best of them in terms of both temperament and intellectual preparation. For all of these reasons, I wholeheartedly support his educational goals and his application to your graduate program.

Sincerely,

Fairview Heights Hospital

To Whom It May Concern:

As the Head of the Nursing Department at Fairview Heights Hospital, I work with many young volunteers who are considering a career in health care. Occasionally, one comes along whose personality is so unique and outstanding that it becomes truly a joy and privilege to play some part in furthering their career. Brook Scanlan is one of those individuals. I would recommend him very highly as a candidate for your nursing program. In the last five months, he has logged more than 85 volunteer hours, and has become a reliable, favorite face around here.

He first came to our attention as a volunteer in the Pet Therapy program. In January, Brook called us to learn more about the program and its requirements. Subsequently, he had his pet beagle, Chuy, approved as an "animal-assisted activities" dog, and began coming in twice a week to visit patients who were immobile. The two of them were quite a pair—both sweet-tempered and eager to connect. Within a day of his first volunteer shift, Brook knew the name of everybody on our floor, and everybody knew his. Brook and Chuy brought smiles to the faces of many patients.

They created a new set of happy memories for one elderly patient in particular. Mr. Ronald Sinclair, who was hospitalized for complications relating to diabetes, was overwhelmed with emotion when Chuy licked his hands and face. He mentioned that Chuy brought back fond memories of his first seeing-eye dog—also a beagle—named Blitz; he told Brook that Blitz had liked to listen to Broadway showtunes as much as he did; he would even bark in rhythm to the songs. The next time Brook came in to do his pet therapy rounds, he brought a set of tiny speakers and an iPod full of showtunes to Mr. Sinclair's room. The strains of music attracted others on the floor, and several of the nursing staff stopped by to see what all the commotion was about. We all soon discovered that Chuy did not have the same musical sensibility as Mr. Sinclair's late lamented Blitz, but the old man was delighted with the experiment and very touched by the gesture. I think this anecdote shows Brook's thoughtful, generous spirit.

We were surprised and pleased when Brook asked to expand his volunteer work beyond the Pet Therapy program. We promptly put him to work greeting and assisting new patients, working the Library Cart, transporting patients to chapel services, delivering flower arrangements, taking patients outside for fresh air as well as other miscellaneous duties to assist nursing staff. Later, he took on additional duties for Food Services, obtaining information from patients regarding their dietary needs. It's not exaggerating to say that people brighten up when Brook comes into the room—and I'm not simply talking about the patients. On an average day, he rotates between assisting our nursing staff in both the Family Birth Center and Medical Rehabilitation; it's not uncommon for nurses and physician assistants to ask me whether Brook is on shift in their department that day. They always look a little disappointed if the answer is no.

Once, I asked Brook to hold the hand of a patient while I performed venipuncture for blood sampling; he knew that she was not only needlephobic but also very nervous about the possible results of the blood test, so he tossed off a series of corny riddles to keep the mood light. Despite her very real fear of the needle, the patient was distracted enough to smile weakly, and even managed to offer up a joke of her own. An outsider might have thought that Brook was just being silly, but we understood and appreciated the unmistakable intention behind his clowning: to alleviate the patient's fear and discomfort. He is sunny and mischievous, but also perceptive, compassionate and supportive.

When Brook first told me that he was planning to pursue a career in nursing, I quizzed him to make sure he knew what he was getting into. For example, I asked him, "Why wouldn't you want to go to medical school and become a physician instead?" He replied simply: "Patients talk to nurses."

If it's true that people don't remember what you say or do but they never forget how you made them feel, then plenty of our patients will associate warmth and laughter with the name Brook Scanlan.

His academic letters of recommendation will tell you what you need to know about his intellectual preparation and thirst for learning; I can only tell you about his excellent bedside manner. He moves naturally and confidently in this environment. It is so easy to picture him brightening the lives of patients in the future. He has an unsinkable optimism, an admirable work ethic, and a genuine desire to connect with the people he comes into contact with. This combination of traits is a winning one. I urge you to accept him into your nursing program.

Sincerely,

Southern University

Psychology Department

215 Admissions Office
2081 Viking Way
Houston, Texas 77001

To Whom It May Concern:

Last summer, I served as the graduate student instructor for Psychology 190: Developmental Psychology, a course taught by Professor Chaim Levin, who is cosigning this letter. It was at that time that I became acquainted with Emelinda Acuña, whose intellectual drive and personal character greatly impressed me as being very well suited for graduate study. When she told me of her plans to study dentistry, and asked me for a letter, I was delighted to have the opportunity to support her application. Of all the undergraduate students for whom I have written recommendations, she stands out as a unique and appealing amalgam of intellectual curiosity and personal tenacity. She holds herself to uncompromisingly high standards and has proved herself unafraid of hard work.

The grading structure of the course was as follows: 1) 10% for attendance and participation 2) 60% for exams and quizzes 3) 15% for a case study observation project and write-up 4) 15% for a final project relating to psychology research design.

In all of my interactions with Ms. Acuña, I found her to be a deeply serious student. In hindsight, then, it is doubly surprising that she stumbled so badly on the first midterm, earning a 68. Instead of resigning herself to a lower grade in the class, Ms. Acuña clearly redoubled her study efforts, because she earned A's and A–'s on all subsequent exams and quizzes. She became a regular face at midterm review sessions, and sought me out occasionally after lecture to ask questions. When she asked about extra credit to make back points she had lost on the first midterm, Professor Levin and I told her that if she were willing to participate in Psychology Human Participant Pool research experiments (1 point per experiment) and by writing two-page reaction papers to relevant journal articles (2 points per write-up). Most students decline the second option, but Ms. Acuña leaped at the opportunity. Any additional time spent learning about pediatric psychology, she said, would only increase her preparation for dental school and her future career. Over the course of the semester, Ms. Acuña earned 20 extra credit points (the maximum allowed) by participating in two graduate student psychology experiments and writing nine reaction papers. I found her observations on the academic papers to be succinct and incisive; as it turns out, she took them very seriously because she was already planning to incorporate them into her final project.

About halfway through the semester, I went to the Child Emotion Lab one day to test the software for my own research project and noticed Ms. Acuña waiting to be called in take part in the research experiment of one of my colleagues. She saw me setting up the computers and offered to help; while we calibrated the experimental settings, we had the chance to chat at length about the journal articles she had been reviewing as part of her extra credit assignments; I was tickled to learn that all of the journal articles she had chosen to related to child psychology issues in pediatric medicine or dentistry. She reported that she was learning a lot about research methodology by reading so many studies. She also mentioned a few topics she'd been considering for her research design proposal. I steered her away from the more impractical options, but found intriguing her references to a group of studies addressing various aspects of gender differences in dental phobia as well as pain sensitivity, and related topics, such as the influence of maternal reactions, social learning and manipulation of expectations. I offered her a few suggestions to help her refine the topic and objectives of a proper lab project.

Ultimately, the title of her proposed research project was: "Dental Anxiety: Correlations to Pain Sensitivity, Gender and Age of Onset in Healthy Children." The project proposal was well thought-out and her review of literature—unsurprisingly—more comprehensive and detailed than nearly any other student's. Dr. Levin agreed with me that the proposal warranted an A; he even encouraged Ms. Acuña to consider applying for an undergraduate research stipend so that she could actually test her hypothesis in an experimental setting. As I understand it, Ms. Acuña did just that; she asked Dr. Millikin, a Psychology faculty member whose research interests include anxiety disorders, to be her preceptor—and she is currently awaiting approval of her funding request.

I believe she will pursue this line of research in the future; I encouraged her to investigate graduate programs that would allow her the option of doing independent research during her dental studies. Ms. Acuña is intent on eventually establishing her own practice in pediatric and family dentistry, and I have no doubt that she will be the type of health care professional who stays rigorously up-to-date on the latest research and applies those principles to make the dental visit as comfortable as possible for her patients. She has the intellectual profile and motivation to succeed brilliantly in dental school, and therefore I can recommend her without reservation for your program.

Sincerely,

Anna York   Dr. Chaim Levin

Wilmington Veterans Administration Hospital

To Whom It May Concern:

I am the Assistant Director of the Freeman Eye Clinic of the Wilmington Veterans Administration Hospital, but I write this letter on behalf of our entire clinic staff to acknowledge Nathan Jarvis's work as an optometric assistant, and to highly recommend him for your O.D. program.

I am a graduate of the Pacific University College of Optometry in Oregon (1986), a member of the American Academy of Optometry and the American Optometric Association, and board certified in both Delaware and Pennsylvania. I have employed and mentored many young pre-optometry students over the past twenty years, and Nathan Jarvis stands out as one of the more unusual applicants.

Over the past year, Nathan's responsibilities and on-the-job training have included visual testing, frame and lens dispensing, front office skills, and administrative tasks. He quickly developed competence with these various technical and clinical duties. I prefer to hire optometric assistants who are planning to pursue a career as an O.D., and I pride myself on putting them through their paces; I make sure that they understand all the science behind the stereopsis and lensometry. It is clear to me from our interactions that Nathan's scientific aptitude is robust and well-grounded.

Nathan also has great front office skills. Not only does he possess a professional, friendly manner, but he is quite happy to explain the ocular testing machines or the anatomy of the eye to patients in clear, accessible language. In fact, Nathan even successfully helped a couple of panicked patients (who were calling from home) to find the contact lens that they dropped, by offering helpful suggestions over the phone on where to look.

What's most striking about Nathan, however, is his interest in the larger field, as evidenced by the initiative he has taken to gain experience with both clinical research and vision care health policy. When we were hiring for this position, Nathan inquired about our involvement with clinical trials, explaining that he was deeply interested in gaining firsthand experience with this aspect of research.

We are currently involved in two large-scale Phase III clinical trials: the first, sponsored by the National Eye Institute and Pfizer, Inc., is evaluating the efficacy of a new drug called Sorbinil in preventing eye and nerve damage in people with diabetes; the second one, backed by ISTA Pharmaceuticals, is testing a new proprietary once-daily formulation of XibromTM (bromfenac ophthalmic solution) for the treatment of pain and inflammation following cataract surgery.

The guidelines regulating who can actually explain the protocol, risks or epidemiological outcomes to participants are, naturally, quite strict. Nathan lacks the scientific training or credentials to interact as deeply with trial participants as he would like. But when he made it clear that he wanted to learn as much as he could about the trials process, we delegated some of the auxiliary administrative duties to him, such as tracking the inventory of the medications in question, collating various questionnaires for newly enrolled participants, and organizing the files and patient histories of trial participants. In short, he has taken over a lot of the administrative tasks related to our office's involvement with these research trials. Nathan has also taken advantage of the Sorbinil trial coordinator's site visits to our clinic to ask about the progress of the study. I believe she was impressed by his questions and his interest. He is gaining invaluable experience in the procedural logistics of coordinating and implementing clinical research trials, should he choose to pursue that avenue in the future. After all, it seems to fall under the category of what truly excites him.

The vast majority of the optometric assistants I've worked with over the years have shown keen interest in honing their clinical and technical skills. Because I keep in touch with them, I know that their potential has been borne out as they proceed to earn their O.D. degrees and set up their own successful practices; one or two have pursued the path of opthalmologic surgery. These others aspire to restore or correct vision for individual patients, one by one. Nathan would make an exceptional optometrist, but he stands out because he wants to be involved in larger-scale developments that will impact scores of eyecare patients. He wants to be involved with the most innovative medications, products, and equipment—but he is also quite passionate about issues surrounding social access to basic eyecare services. In my experience, it's unusual for somebody so young to exhibit such professional focus—and especially the interest in institutional and systemic level long-term outcomes. For example, I understand that he is currently applying for an data analyst internship with the Center for Vision Care Policy and Research. I am not sure whether Nathan will eventually become a medical researcher or a policy researcher, but it's clear that his academic background (he's a Sociology major and a Mathematics minor) will stand him in good stead for either career.

In summary, Nathan has the analytical aptitude, the intellectual curiosity, and the communication skills to succeed in any aspect of optometry that he chooses to pursue. He also cares about the long-term improvement of the field for the patients and has demonstrated through concrete action his commitment to high quality care. Nathan Jarvis is the kind of knowledgeable, well-rounded candidate who would be an asset to any optometry school.

Sincerely,

HERMAN PRATHER ANIMAL HOSPITAL
CINCINNATI ZOO

To Whom It May Concern:

I am offering Haesong Im my highest recommendation for veterinary school because I sincerely believe that he deserves the opportunity to get the advanced training he seeks. Since his academic record—and his GRE score in particular—may not adequately indicate his ability to succeed in veterinary school, I would like to document the list of his qualities that do speak to his professional potential. I am the Deputy Veterinarian at the Herman Prather Animal Hospital at the Cincinnati Zoo. I did my training at the University of Guelph ('87) and have previously worked at the Cleveland Metroparks Zoo as well as the Wildlife Conservation Society.

Having served on a vet school admissions committee myself, I know as well as you do that while high grade point averages and GRE test scores have been statistically correlated to early success in graduate school, they don't tell the whole story; other factors, such as extensive clinical experience, are equally as important. The field abounds with gifted veterinarians whose skill at connecting with their animal patients more than makes up for a lackluster undergraduate GPA.

Zoo nursery attendant is a very popular job; when we advertised for this position last year, we were flooded with resumes; most of the applicants were recent college grads who were book-smart but experience-poor. They had tons of pre-vet coursework but very little hands-on experience with animals, especially with non-domesticated species. We hired Haesong on the strength of his previous work experience with wild animals: as an undergraduate, he had elected to do a field study at the Mardell Game Preserve, where he helped veterinarians electronically tag and track small game, big game, and waterfowl.

Haesong helps us care for newborn and young animals in the Cincinnati Zoo nursery and exhibit area. He prepares sterilized nursing bottles with liquid formula, cereal, and regular vitamin supplements for young animals according to my direction and prepares standard diet foods for mothers of newborn animals according to the requirements of its species. He hand-feeds animals that have been orphaned or deserted, or that require food in addition to that provided by their mothers. Sometimes an animal in our care will inexplicably reject the formula or food, and Haesong takes the finicky eaters under his care. I have seen him spend hours at the blender, experimenting with different combinations—all containing the same prescribed ratio of protein to carbs—until he stumbles upon the flavor cocktail that works. His tireless efforts have helped many an underweight, undernourished baby animal regain its zest for eating.

He conducts physical examinations of the young animals, taking temperatures, blood pressure, and pulse rate, and weighing and measuring them. Because he monitors and records vital signs with a specificity beyond what is strictly mandated, Haesong has occasionally detected indications of abnormality or disease at a very early stage, and alerts me or the other veterinary staff that the animal in question may need special attention.

His memory for numbers and statistics is quite remarkable, as is his problem-solving acumen. These talents are paired with a laidback, low-key manner that our animal patients respond to. Even during crises and moments of great stress, Haesong keeps his cool; I can recall many instances when an animal was brought to us in critical condition that he was able to assist us ably and efficiently.

Another aspect of his job involves dealing with the public. Schoolchildren on field trips always bombard us with questions about the procedures for care and feeding of young animals. Haesong seems to genuinely enjoy this duty, and the staff has nominated him to be our default point-man to answer their questions. Also, thanks to his prior experience at the Mardell Game Preserve, Haesong is able to provide visitors with firsthand and species-specific knowledge about many animals' native habitats and breeding habits. Haesong has even joined us on camera for various Animal Planet shows such as "Wild Rescues" to explain the feeding and sleeping habits of his charges.

His bedside manner is impeccable. For example, he has developed a knack for holding the bottle just so for feeding the baby wombats without giving them gas. At our year-end banquet, we awarded him the honorary title of "Wombat Whisperer." He wears it proudly.

All admissions committees leave a few seats open for applicants whose quantitative criteria fall below the mean. Mr. Im is the type of applicant that you make exceptions for. Not only has he worked in several areas of the veterinary medical profession, gaining exposure to an impressive portfolio of species in the process, but he has the maturity, communication skills, and absolute commitment to care that characterizes the best veterinarians I know. There is no substitute for experience; it proves character, heart, grit, and agility of mind. Haesong Im has all of these traits. I urge you to offer him an opportunity to interview so that you can meet him in person and judge for yourself.

Sincerely,

Fordham University
New York

To Whom It May Concern:

Every year, approximately 50 students request that I write a letter of recommendation for them; after examining their records and the materials they have provided me, I turn down about 50% of the requests so that I can write letters of substance for the remaining students, whom I feel show special promise. Sarah McSweeney is one of those individuals. Having taught in the Anthropology department of Fordham University for ten years, I would rate Ms. McSweeney in the top 5% of all undergraduate students who have taken my classes. I can assure you that she will be a credit to your law school, as I have reason to believe that her thirst to succeed is unusual, tenacious and very deeply rooted.

Sarah McSweeney took two of my courses: "Introduction to Ethnography," in Fall Semester of last year (final grade: B), and "Anthropology of Education" this Fall Semester (final grade: A+). Her performance in the first course was—in a word—undistinguished; in fact, in preparing to write this letter, I asked my "Introduction to Ethnography" teaching assistant for his impression of Ms. McSweeney. He told me that he barely remembered her; she had never spoken up in class. This surprised me immensely because by now I cannot imagine Ms. McSweeney as anything but the determined, engaged student whose hand is always raised in class because she wants to clarify a point or draw a connection to an assigned reading.

When I asked Ms. McSweeney what had motivated her remarkable academic improvement, she explained that she'd had a near-death experience last winter that caused her to reexamine her priorities. I will allow her to describe the particulars of that epiphany for you in her personal statement, but I consider it my duty to call your attention to the effect it has had on her transcript: within the space of two semesters, she has transformed herself from a slightly above-average student into a stellar academic performer.

In short, Ms. McSweeney's academic performance in "Anthropology of Education" has been exceptional. In a class of 60 students, Ms. McSweeney's rank is #1. Her superior performance is a direct result of her fearless commitment to asking questions and taking intellectual risks.

For this particular course, 65% of a student's grade is tied up with the Field Project, an ethnographic study of an educational fieldsite. Ms. McSweeney identified a local school district that is teaching Connected Math (sometimes described as "anti-racist mathematics") as part of its curricular reform and restructuring; more specifically, she focused her observations on the parents group, Community Support for Traditional Educational Concepts (CSTEC), that is lobbying the local school board to revoke the teaching of Connected Math. Essentially, she chose to focus on the curriculum battles as a site of ritual conflict, continuity and discontinuity, power relations, and core symbols. Her final write-up laid out a cogent analysis of how, when culturally different models are being constituted as the students' first introduction to geometry or algebra, parents who resist the new math are alienated from their own sense of educational ritual and the scientific universals underlying some of their most basic assumptions about reality; her most intriguing turn involves citing Willard Berman's work on race privilege to suggest that the CSTEC members' resentment derives from being turned into unwitting and unwilling outsiders of the group where they used to hold privileged insider status, in effect, that they are being forced to take an detached "ethnographic" view of the unstated power relations and cultural practices within their own once-familiar domain.

Ms. McSweeney's argument is admirably multivalenced and quite thought-provoking. I enjoyed the process of helping her develop her thesis when she brought early drafts to me, and I have encouraged her to revise and expand the paper with a view towards presenting her work at an undergraduate research symposium.

In more than two decades of teaching, I have often encountered students who have displayed academic improvement, but rarely one who seems to have attacked the project with such energy. Ms. McSweeney tells me that the next goals on her list are to attend a prestigious law school, specialize in constitutional law, and eventually be appointed to a judgeship. She is a woman of unstoppable momentum; given what she has been through, I daresay that no setbacks will hold her back for long.

If your law program is seeking a candidate with a vibrant intellect, articulated ambition, and unshakeable will, you need look no further than Ms. McSweeney. She has my highest recommendation.

Sincerely,

UNIVERSITY OF NORTH NEVADA

POLITICAL SCIENCE DEPARTMENT

To Whom It May Concern:

It is particularly gratifying for me to write in support of Jeremiah Townsend's application to your law school, as I am the professor who was apparently responsible in part for Mr. Townsend discovering his interest in—and aptitude for—pursuing a legal career. Mr. Townsend enrolled in my class as a Computer Science major who needed to fulfill a graduation breadth requirement; he concluded it intent on pursuing a career in Intellectual Property Law. I would rate him in the top 5% of all students that I have taught over the past ten years, and in the top 2% of pre-law students whom I have recommended.

I hold a Ph.D. in Political Science and a J.D. from Georgetown University, and I have published papers and taught classes on e-business and new media law issues. I helped draft an amicus brief last year for the *Perfect 10 v. Google, Inc.* case pending in the U.S. Ninth Circuit Court. It was one of the texts that I assigned as background reading for a debate for students in my course, "New Media and the Courts." Jeremiah originally came into my office hours to "protest" being assigned to the anti-Google side. It sparked a lively conversation, and I was so taken with this young man's line of questioning that we continued the conversation over coffee. His Computer Science major predisposed him initially towards a very enthusiastic pro-technology stance. During lecture, I remember, Mr. Townsend would often express a very libertarian stance towards online privacy issues and file-sharing technology. Like the vast majority of his Generation Y (a.k.a. "Generation Wired") peers, his mantra was: Information wants to be free. However, he was slowly growing into a more mature and nuanced view. As a student consultant for a digital archiving project at the library, he was seeing firsthand how media migration exposed the limitations of unfettered progress, at least insofar as it outstripped the social capacity to keep up. His idealism was being tempered by reality. Far from rejecting the newfound complexity, he declared it confusing but exciting. I encouraged him to explore this tension in his term paper.

The thesis he eventually formulated set out to debunk the argument that Google Print qualifies as a realistic textual preservation effort; he also questioned the impact the Google Print project would have on fair use and the funding of other non-Google digitization projects. It was a complex argument, and I saw it as a sign of his intellectual growth.

Considering his lack of background in political science, it would also be quite a feat to pull it off. Recognizing that he didn't feel comfortable with the writing process and especially handling the caselaw, Mr. Townsend asked me and his TA to look over several early drafts of the paper. He learned with remarkable rapidity to find relevant legal citations and commentaries, and then to quickly determine the usefulness of an article and how it fit with the rest of the information he had already gathered. His learning curve was steep but he attacked it with vigor. The final draft touched on digital format obsolescence, the Creative Commons and copyright caselaw, library exceptionalism and copyright maximalism. It was a well-organized synthesis of diverse sources, and displayed intelligent close readings and analysis. I considered it a triumph for dogged determination and supple intellect in equal measure.

Mr. Townsend told me later that the experience of researching and writing the paper was the impetus for studying law. He presented a revised and expanded version of that term paper at an undergraduate research symposium, declared a minor in Political Science, and began preparing for the LSAT. He also became a member of the Pre-Law Club and volunteered to coordinate a series of talks on IP issues, inviting speakers to address student audiences on topics ranging from file-sharing to virtual libel. In the spirit of freeing information, Mr. Townsend made the talks available (with permission, of course) as podcasts on his website and published the transcripts in the Pre-Law Club's online newsletter.

Mr. Townsend has expressed aspirations of using his J.D. to work as a lobbyist for the Electronic Frontier Federation or some other such non-profit. I can just as easily see him making partner in an IP firm or serving as in-house counsel for a Silicon Valley tech firm.

Whatever path he chooses, his bona fides in technology will serve him in good stead. Jeremiah excels in Computer Science because he enjoys challenges and has a talent for thinking methodically and systematically. The ease with which he was able to gain fluency in social scientific and basic legal reasoning suggests that he had already built an excellent analytical foundation. He is no stranger to thought architecture and logic design. His approach to research was so comprehensive that he could argue either side of the debate.

The field of Intellectual Property Law needs scientists who can anticipate the dynamic development of our increasingly online reality. In Jeremiah Townsend you will find an individual who understands the importance of protecting privacy and proprietary interests as much as he wants to incubate innovation and foster democratic access to information. He has my highest recommendation.

Sincerely,

Albert Williams

Press Secretary – U.S. Congressional District, (Texas 9th), Washington Office
425 Cannon House Office Building
Washington, D.C. 20515-4309

To Whom It May Concern:

With great enthusiasm, I write this letter supporting Mr. Jojo Zolina's application to your law program. He has served as Press Assistant for the last three years under my direct supervision. I am the Press Secretary for Hoffman Cheever, the Representative for Texas's 9th U.S. Congressional District. As the Congressman's initial point of contact with the media, I am responsible for developing strategies to convey the Congressman's policies and positions to the public, handling day-to-day press inquiries and setting up interviews, reviewing and rewriting speeches, staging press conferences, coordinating with other government press offices, and supervising internal and external agency publications. I also coordinate with the communications director in planning and managing media campaigns to put out a consistent long-term message.

As the senior member of my three-person staff, Jojo supports me in some measure with all of these duties. More specifically, he specializes in handling issues related to print media agencies (including web-based publications) and coordinates with our webmaster to keep the "Press Room" section of our website up-to-date. On a typical day, Jojo is one of the first to arrive at the office. By the time I come in at 8 a.m., he has usually already skimmed all the newspapers from our home district and compiled a set of media clips for me to review. When he first started, he was responsible for monitoring political blogs, a nascent media presence; when blogs began to proliferate, however, I passed that task along to a junior staffer because I felt that Jojo's time and skills were better used in writing. Needless to say, he has an excellent way with words. Jojo has a gift for simplifying complicated policy issues into clear and concise bullet points. His ability for turning out clean copy very quickly has been a godsend, considering our stringent deadlines. I now trust him with the first draft of all press releases, pitch letters, media advisories, talking points, and backgrounders. He has also played an instrumental role in training the newest Press Assistants and coached them to accomplish their tasks with the same discretion and critical thinking that I have come to take for granted in him.

Jojo first joined our team in 200x as a campaign volunteer. Not satisfied with the menial work that they had assigned him, he requested a meeting with me, saying that his experience in both journalism and public relations would help us place stories in online and alternative media. He quickly impressed me with his intellect, his diligence and dedication as well as his political instincts. The position often required long hours and weekend work, but I never heard complaints. In fact, Jojo was usually the one trying to keep things light among the other campaign staffers whenever we had to do an all-nighter. He is one of those fortunate people who can operate splendidly on four or five hours of sleep a night. Jojo's untiring efforts freed me up to concentrate on setting the tone and message of the campaign during those crucial last weeks.

More recently, he came to the rescue again. Last summer, I had to take two week's leave to handle a family emergency abroad. It came up quite suddenly, and I wasn't able to give Jojo more than a day's notice that he would have to take over the bulk of my responsibilities. It required him to step up and assume several duties that I had never delegated to him before, such as drafting radio actualities, speechwriting and of course, briefing Congressman Cheever directly on press coverage, news developments, the daily "message," and potential media reaction to proposed policies. Jojo and I phone-conferenced several times a day; I reviewed the most important speeches and scripts and faxed back my revisions. However, there was a limit to how much attention I could spare, and for all intents and purposes, Jojo performed 90% of my job for that fortnight.

My faith in his ability to learn on the fly was borne out, though it did prove to be a learning experience for him. One of the first things I'd taught him was to always assume he was speaking "on the record" and therefore to never feel obligated to answer a reporter's question immediately. During those two weeks, when he stepped into my shoes, I cautioned him to have one of the other press assistants filter all his calls. However, because he was so habituated to answer calls (i.e. to screen them for me), and because he had established relationships with these reporters, Jojo slipped up and gave a statement that he later had to retract. As press blunders go, it was truly minor, but a valuable lesson nonetheless. At my insistence, Jojo called up the reporter to admonish her for misquoting him and to reset their professional relationship. Although he had cultivated wonderfully cordial relations with reporters up to that point, this incident really impressed upon him the delicate political dance of establishing genuine trust with agents of the press while simultaneously keeping a necessary distance. Congressman Cheever told me that he thought Jojo did a very competent job during those pressure-filled weeks.

What I truly appreciate is Jojo's sixth sense for anticipating my needs and planning accordingly. For example, I know that if breaking news happens while I am in a meeting, by the time I come back to the office, Jojo will have already drafted a response or a set of talking points. On at least five or six separate occasions, he read the statement to me over the phone, got my approval, and transmitted it to reporters before their evening deadlines so that it could make the next news cycle.

In general, and especially on occasions when we find ourselves in a media frenzy, I can trust Jojo to respond very promptly and to be judicious in prioritizing the demands placed upon him. However, this office is also indebted to Jojo for an initiative that involved long-range media strategy. After the 200x election, he spoke up about increasing our media presence in the district's Asian American community—not only because that population had experienced sizable growth since the last census, but because exit polling suggested that they had an unfavorable impression of Congressman Cheever. Jojo strongly advocated that we consider hiring somebody with more specialized language skills—someone who could help us monitor our coverage in Chinese-language media as well as translate our press releases into Chinese to reach more of our constituents in that community. I agreed, and our next intern hire targeted those specific skills. Jojo gladly took on the role of training that intern in the required press office skills. Polling from late last year suggests that we have made inroads with Chinese voters, and I honestly believe that Jojo deserves substantial credit for those successes.

In short, I highly recommend Mr. Jojo Zolina for your law program. He is quick-witted, well-spoken, ambitious and well-versed in politics and policy. Classmates will find him collegial and generous with his time, and professors will find the quality of his analysis and writing quite laudable. If you have additional questions about Mr. Zolina's qualifications, I would be more than happy to elaborate.

Sincerely,

TITAN BANCORP

To Whom It May Concern:

I am the Assistant General Counsel (Legal Dept. – Litigation) at Titan Bancorp, a Fortune 500 commercial bank. I have known Mr. Abdallah Najjar for four years and have been impressed by his work ethic, sharp intellect and general excellence as a paralegal in two separate workplaces. In fact, if my role as his supervising attorney had not made me the logical choice to be the one recommending him to your law school, I would have submitted a peer letter of reference—so strongly do I believe in supporting his career. In my opinion, Mr. Najjar has amply demonstrated his capacity to handle the rigors of law school and ultimately law practice.

I first met Abdallah Najjar when I was employed as an associate at Bittweiler, Chase & Moncton in Denver. As a corporate paralegal assigned to the Contracts department, where I worked, he often assisted me with due diligence projects: organizing minute books, summarizing board resolutions, and conducting research. He coordinated corporate closings for which he was responsible for tracking reams of documents, ensuring that each one was executed by the correct parties, and distributing closing sets to all parties. Mr. Najjar was a godsend to me at that firm; not only did he work well under pressure, but he was also utterly reliable. I knew that any task that I delegated to him would be completed with the same meticulous attention to detail that I would have demanded of myself.

Since we were roughly the same age and shared an interest in politics, we would often chat over lunch; we even attended a few social events together. Even after I left Bittweiler, Chase & Moncton in order to take a position as an assistant in-house counsel at Titan, Mr. Najjar and I kept in occasional touch. I knew that he was increasingly dissatisfied with the lack of intellectual challenge in his assignments, and that he did not see opportunity for continued growth at the firm. He also wanted to gain exposure to different practice areas, and had a particular interest in litigation. When my new firm announced that it was planning to expand its paralegal staff, it felt completely natural for me to encourage Mr. Najjar to apply for the job.

Although I was not involved in the hiring decision, I was told later that they had picked Mr. Najjar in large part because of his initiative and ambition; he had recently gained certification in Civil Litigation and E-discovery through NALA (National Association for Legal Assistants) continuing education courses. Those new competencies of his were put to the test as soon as he was hired. We were at the time swamped with a massive overhaul of the corporate pension plan as well as a series of wrongful termination suits. Mr. Najjar was thrust into the fray, required to tackle multiple demanding tasks in an incredibly fast-paced environment with no substantive training; the rest of the office was too busy to orient him properly. That month, everybody had to work 70-hour weeks. Even though Mr. Najjar had recently gotten married, he bore the overtime burden uncomplainingly. Both in terms of work quality and team spirit, he exceeded our expectations. The other supervising attorneys were surprised; I was merely impressed all over again.

Truth be told, I'd rather missed working with a paralegal who had a knack for anticipating what we lawyers needed. This is the kind of prescience only comes from studying the workflow and the people involved. Even in the whirlwind pressure of overwork, Mr. Najjar had been able to assimilate the "dependencies" between project team members in a very systematic way—and use that information to help him prioritize and meet deadlines.

His daily workload as a litigation paralegal involves analyzing and summarizing complex pleadings, performing discovery, interviewing clients and gathering evidence that will counter direct allegations or assumptions in pleadings. He performs these tasks with accuracy and with all due consideration for internal and external stakeholders.

The higher the quality of the paralegal staff, the easier it is for the in-house litigator to take on additional litigation matters without a decline in the manner in which he handles each case. Considering that the legal responsibility for a paralegal's work rests directly and solely upon the lawyers, it is no small testament to Mr. Najjar's competence that our department has entrusted him with ever more responsibility. His exposure to client contact has increased to the point where the firm trusts him to handle small claims cases and settlements independently.

He meets the highest ethical standards and rules of professional responsibility, managing sensitive documents and materials with scrupulous confidentiality. Mr. Najjar possesses excellent writing and analytical skills as well as the ability to handle difficult situations with tact and professionalism. I have personally witnessed him responding with incredible poise and maturity to confrontational clients as well as a senior attorney who had a habit of verbally abusing the administrative staff.

I believe that Mr. Najjar's current position has provided him the challenge that he was seeking; on a daily basis, he handles multiple cases with varying complex issues, interacts extensively with clients, drafts pleadings and argues his position both verbally and in writing. He has assisted me, my colleagues, and my superiors superbly. Now that he has decided that the time has come for him to embrace new challenges. Far from begrudging him the opportunity to advance his career, I am determined to offer my complete support. It is completely obvious to me that Mr. Najjar possesses the skills and determination to handle the rigors of law school and ultimately law practice. I recommend him for law school without reservations.

Sincerely,

St. Brendan Catholic Worker House

To Whom It May Concern:

My name is Marie Valdez and I am the manager of the St. Brendan Catholic Worker House. I write this letter to offer my testimony to Clark Kinkead's character, his sense of mission and his gift for expression as he tenders his application to law school. I can give personal assurances as to Clark's organizational and time management skills, not to mention the passion for social justice issues that he has been able to explore and deepen through lay ministries and campaigns. I only hope that my words convey the surety of my conviction that he deserves this opportunity at your institution. Clark is, I would imagine, older than most of your applicants—and already possessed of an established, successful career; these factors would deter many from taking on the personal upheaval of starting over professionally. In Clark, these factors only speak to the depth of his commitment to study law so that he can more fully serve society.

I have known Clark for nine years as a fellow parishioner at Our Lady of the Pillar Catholic Church; however, I have gotten to know him much more deeply over the last two years, since he started volunteering at our Catholic Worker chapter house. We are a gospel-based community committed to the daily practice of the works of mercy – feeding the hungry, sheltering the homeless, visiting the imprisoned, and comforting the sorrowful. Grounded in a firm belief in the God-given dignity of every human person, we distribute food, hold prayer vigils and nonviolent direct action against the death penalty and militarism, coordinate a hospice program and do street outreach ministry for men who are addicted and coming out of jail. We are located in a section of town that has slowly become blighted by poverty and open drug abuse, and we strive to offer a hospitable refuge from despair, addiction and violence of the street culture.

Clark first came to help out on a food pantry project that his wife was involved with; he was drawn back, I believe, by the warmth of fellowship and the satisfaction of service. Through his initial work with the food pantry, Clark met several homeless vets who were struggling with substance abuse. These were men who had all individually made several attempts to quit using heroin. As Clark got to know them, he learned about the shortage of beds in drug treatment centers and came to deplore the fact that the number of beds in new and planned prisons outnumbered those in rehabilitation centers. The men's stories of their experience in prison quickened Clark's conviction that the laws surrounding drug-related offenses needed to change to favor medical intervention and rehabilitation over punitive measures, such as the harsh automatic sentencing standards for drug offenders in our state.

During one of our weekly community roundtable discussions, Clark stood up and spoke passionately about the need to institute more harm reduction measures. I was so impressed with his fervor that I asked him if he would be willing to speak at the rally at the Capitol that the Catholic Worker was helping to organize; the rally was to show support for Proposition 19, a citizen-initiated initiative modeled after the measure that passed successfully in California several years ago. It would allow most people convicted of first- and second-time nonviolent, simple drug possession to receive drug treatment instead of incarceration. At first, Clark demurred because he felt that expressing his beliefs on a controversial topic in such a public forum could adversely affect his business if his clients saw him on television or read about him in the newspaper. I respected his wishes and did not press him. A few days later, Clark emailed me to say he had changed his mind; several conversations with his wife had convinced him that he was allowing material considerations to censor himself from doing good in the world.

I believe that was the moment that he started wondering whether he wanted to continue with a livelihood that would always ask him to be more circumspect than he felt himself becoming. The more he learned about the issues that impacted the marginalized populations in our community, the more he was driven to action. His faith was maturing, growing hand-in-hand with his need to speak his mind on social justice issues. Later that year, he organized a teach-in on the efficacy of needle exchange and safe injection sites as they have been implemented in other countries. He has also become increasingly involved in working with other non-profit organizations to call for investigations into recent allegations of police brutality. He is a bright presence in our community.

Clark has worked as a financial planner for the past fifteen years. During one of our conversations, I discovered that he had been a Political Science major in college; even then, he had been interested in continuing on to law school, but his parents had pressed him to follow in the family business. If I were to guess as to why his true vocation is welling up so irresistibly now, it would be that he has proven his ability in business; he has satisfied familial obligations and the responsibilities of a householder. It is time for him to follow the path of the heart and spirit.

With a law degree, Clark will be in a position to advocate and implement programs and policies that afford legal options for social equality to former convicts and the underprivileged. He will focus his efforts on challenging and rewriting laws that have effectively served to further marginalize the individuals in our society who have the least amount of hope. I have a profound admiration for Clark's intellect, his mission and his tenacity. I consider myself blessed to count this man as a friend and colleague in Christ. He will make a difference in our community.

I would be glad to elaborate on any issues pertaining to this letter. I can be contacted at (xxx) xxx--xxxx.

Sincerely,

Unger High School

1234 Main St. Augusta, ME 54321

To Whom It May Concern:

I am writing to offer my recommendation of Lauren Maitskill for your Baccalaureate/MBA program. I teach the photojournalism class that produces the *Plume*, Unger High School's annual yearbook, and I believe that Lauren's leadership of the Yearbook staff truly exemplifies her finest traits: her creativity, her pragmatism, and her commitment to excellence. She first came to my attention last year when she did yeoman's work as both a section editor and the assistant Advertising Editor. This year, as the *Plume's* Editor-in-Chief, she has not only helped produce one of the best-looking books on record, but she has also helped chart new directions for the publication that will help ensure its longevity.

In my Yearbook Journalism class, every student is expected to gain competence in photography, writing, production under deadline, and design and layout software. The role of the student editor-in-chief approaches that of a teaching assistant in a college class; although I teach the basics, the editor-in-chief shares responsibility for helping the staff apply those photojournalism skills on a daily basis. Lauren understood that the production process required a total collaborative effort; she consistently delegated tasks in a way that encouraged skill-building; for example, she paired veteran photographers and page designers with their newbie counterparts so that the younger staff members would learn more quickly. When they needed additional coaching and assistance outlining stories and writing headlines, she often gave up her lunch period to sit and work with them—always cheerfully.

Without ever losing sight of the details, she thought about the yearbook from an overall perspective and devised ways to make the book better. The thing that I want to highlight about Lauren is her eagerness to improve the yearbook—and its bottom line—by capitalizing on new technologies. Lauren took a real interest in the business side of the yearbook enterprise. She harbored no sentimental attachments to tradition for the sake of tradition. For example, she wanted to know why yearbook sales have declined in the past few years. She proposed that we commission a survey to find out why—and worked with the newspaper editor to make it happen. Though admittedly unscientific, the resulting poll did suggest that popular online networking sites such as MySpace and Facebook have given students the opportunity to exchange pictures and comment on each other all year round—moreover, for free—thus decreasing the appeal of the yearbook. In response, Lauren proposed that we revamp our *Plume* website to include more social networking features. She also worked with the Advertising Editor and our Webmaster to institute a pilot program where our advertisers were given the option of buying year-round online ads. The experiment paid off financially, and we plan to expand it next year.

Lastly, Lauren initiated a class discussion on the topic of new media; it was a lively debate that generated interesting insights. The general conclusion: because the prevalence of digital camera and cell phone cameras has turned average students into amateur photographers, the value of a physical photo album that encapsulates their high school experience—i.e. the Yearbook—is losing its appeal. Lauren became intent on bringing back our medium's uniqueness; one of her strategies was to raise the quality of our photojournalism by reminding everybody to hew to the formal principles of photographic composition so that our pictures would look more professional—but also to experiment so that the images would be more eye-catching.

As you will see from her application, Lauren Maitskill is a student of many talents. She has maintained a 4.1 GPA while playing varsity badminton and intramural soccer. In addition to excelling in academics and athletics, Lauren has also devoted herself to volunteer work with Big Sisters, the Red Cross, and numerous campus clubs. It is obvious to me that being able to pursue diverse interests has made Lauren a better yearbook editor and a well-rounded human being.

I generally discourage students from applying to accelerated or compressed degree programs; I believe that college students should have the space to explore electives before they commit to one field of study. In ten years of teaching, only two or three other students have asked me to recommend them for five-year Baccalaureate/MBA programs, and I declined, quite frankly because I did not see them thriving in such a program. I have made an exception in writing this letter for Lauren. It is not simply that she is easily the most business-minded student editor-in-chief I have ever worked with, or that she has assured me that the Baccalaureate/MBA program has a reputation for producing thoughtful, motivated young MBAs. Simply put, I support her application because I believe that her intense pragmatism will prompt her to assess her goals regularly and make the right choices to fit those goals.

Ms. Maitskill is enormously creative, innovative, and resourceful. When she notices something that isn't working, she moves quickly to change it. At the same time, she is willing to study what is working and ask: "How could this be even better?" I see a bright future for her. She will bring great energy and vitality to your program. If I can be of further assistance in discussing Lauren Maitskill's qualifications, please do not hesitate to contact me.

Sincerely,

Genia Energy Consulting

To Whom It May Concern:

This letter provides me the opportunity to recommend my Research Associate, Jeanne Giragosian, for the MBA program at your university. I have been Jeanne's supervising manager at Genia Energy Consulting for the past three years.

Genia provides research, testimony, reports and regulatory support to consumer advocates, environmental organizations, regulatory commissions, state energy offices, and others; we specialize in consulting on energy, economic, and environmental topics. While I wish Jeanne the best and fully understand that she must advance her career, I'm truly sorry to see her go. She has been such a productive member of our team, and such a bright presence in the office.

Jeanne first came to us as a summer intern four years ago. She made a very positive impression on us with her work ethic and avid curiosity. She kept in touch and indicated that she would be very interested in a full-time position with us after she graduated. When we expanded our roster of Research Associates a few months later, she was at the top of our list for new hires. With her bachelor's degree in both Environmental Science and Economics, not to mention her comfort level with our mandate and methods, Jeanne was easily able to get up to speed with the content challenges of the investigations and project reports.

She started as a Research Assistant, but after six months she was promoted to Research Associate, responsible for traveling to field sites, interviewing relevant sources, and writing testimony and reports on a wide range of issues. She has acquitted herself magnificently in this position. Jeanne is an excellent technical writer. She is very meticulous in her approach to research, formatting, and proofreading her reports.

Jeanne is well prepared for the social interplay that is required of any strong manager. She is one of the more sociable staffers at Genia; whenever somebody new comes into the company—and these last two years have seen the firm grow by 25%—Jeanne always takes a leading role in orienting the new hires. In that sense, she was a natural choice to administer the student summer internship that she herself had once participated in. In fact, her performance in this role has influenced the way we orient and train interns and new researchers. In the process of explaining her methodology and writing process to the intern, Jeanne generated a series of informal checklists and a style manual; they realized eventually that they could refine and formalize these protocols for future interns because they proved so useful in accelerating the learning curve. I gladly encouraged them to pursue this side project. Other Research Associates who find themselves working outside of their normal areas of expertise have also made use of these protocols.

Jeanne stands out because she is interested in learning all aspects of our business. Most of our research associates specialize in a handful of topics once they find their niche, e.g. somebody who is well-versed in asset valuation and price forecasting might expand their interests to performance ratemaking or the ratepayer impact of new capacity market structures, but would be unlikely to want to take on the complexities of transmission planning and siting, or the feasibility of carbon sequestration. Early on, however, Jeanne had made a specific request for exposure to several fields and analytical streams, and insofar as I could accommodate her, I have attempted to give her a wide diversity of assignments. Gaining breadth of knowledge requires her to do a great deal more background reading, but she hasn't complained. On the contrary, she truly seems to thrive on achieving a global understanding of these issues. She is a generalist in the finest sense of the word.

As for Jeanne's plans for her post-MBA career, I know that she aspires to work for a firm that offers venture assistance, strategic advice and capital to greentech entrepreneurial ventures. She took a Corporate Finance course through Duke University Extension last spring. I believe that was a turning point for her in deciding that she could best make a difference by supporting sustainable and scalable ventures in biofuel, energy storage and energy conservation. To offer a metaphor: Over the past three years, Jeanne has learned how to assess and redesign well-established gardens and orchards. She does it exceedingly well, but now she realizes that her skills are best suited for the hothouse, where she can assist new gardeners coax exotic seeds into sturdy seedlings. It's important work, and I think the work will suit her exceedingly well.

Jeanne has a rare hunger to learn and a passion for excellence. She has my unequivocal recommendation. I believe she is ready and fully prepared to take on the challenges of an MBA program. If you'd like to discuss her attributes in more detail, please don't hesitate to contact me.

Sincerely,

Play Cube Media

112 4th St. Suite 280
New York, NY 10065

To Whom It May Concern:

It is a distinct pleasure to recommend to you my former employee Louis DiDomenicantonio. In my capacity as founder and CEO of Play Cube Media, an online games company, I worked closely with Louis for four years—and we have remained close even after he left Play Cube to start his own company. As I will explain below, I believe this is the ideal time for Louis to ground his entrepreneurial ambitions with an MBA education. I can also assure you that he will be an energetic, valuable addition to any business school class.

Louis's contributions as Lead Content Designer and Writer were a major factor in our company's success and steady expansion. I had ample opportunity to witness Mr. DiDomenicantonio's range of talents and skills when he helped bring our multiplayer role-playing games RingMistress, The Journey to Zelthacar, and Farmer: The Harrowing all the way from drawing board to market. On his own, he was capable of doing some beautifully detailed design work, including code specification and 3D modeling, but he also brought strong managerial instincts to handling teams (usually of 25-30 people) of artists, programmers, producers, designers, writers and sound engineers. I liked his knack for keeping the team focused and inspired, even when we were running up against tight production deadlines. He gained respect by making everybody feel heard, but was also able to enforce directives and deliver constructive criticism when necessary. People definitely enjoyed working with him; that much was clear. With each additional project, I entrusted him with additional responsibility for running content development meetings, for planning and directing motion-capture shoots and voice recording sessions, and for guaranteeing QA during the testing and revision process. His efforts produced high quality results time and time again.

Consequently, when Play Cube was approached by the Smithkin Graduate School of Management to design a multiplayer business ethics/leadership simulation game for their second-year MBA students, I assigned the project to Louis DiDomenicantonio. I had faith in his ability to lead and manage a stellar team to deliver our client the product they wanted, in the timeframe that they had specified—and as I expected, Louis's ability to design a complex, playable game experience won us plaudits and raves, and a very satisfied customer.

During the early stages of game design, several Smithkin students served as consultants to our game writers on integrating the desired business concepts into the simulations and models. These management-focused individuals were younger than Louis but they had extremely focused business plans; some had already lined up seed funding for their proposed post-MBA ventures. Louis told me later that the experience changed him. It prompted him to revisit his own dormant dreams of starting his own online games company. When I got his letter of resignation a year later, I was not surprised. Unhappy to lose my best designer, yes, but I understood that Louis—whom I considered by now a good friend—felt that he had outgrown the challenges that Play Cube could offer him. As an MBA grad and successful entrepreneur myself, I offered Mr. DiDomenicantonio some friendly advice and support, but the company was his own baby, and he was supremely confident that he would make it succeed.

I'm sure Louis will explain this period in his career in more detail in his application essays and interview, but as I understand it, the company got off to a very promising start, but finances wavered when they overcommitted by taking on a couple of big projects simultaneously; in the end, they didn't completely follow through on either. Mr. DiDomenicantonio had rich experience on the technical and creative side. He also had an excellent eye for talent. However, what he needed—and did not have, at the time—was a viable business model.

Mr. DiDomenicantonio's startup, Four Dog Entertainment, officially went into limbo a few months ago—in some ways, a victim of its own early success. I commiserated with Louis. I also offered him his old job back, but he told me: "Thanks, but I'm going to learn how to do this right." Louis would be a tremendous asset in any software company, but he is apparently determined to be his own boss. I respect and applaud that ambition and grit.

So Mr. DiDomenicantonio will bring that most invaluable resource to share with his business school classmates: his story of failure. As I recall from my own MBA experience, the classmates who had experienced business failures brought the most interesting perspectives—and were often the most motivated to succeed. I can assure you that Louis will attack the curriculum with a ravenous appetite, and that his MBA peers will be delighted by his stories, his insights and his leadership skills.

I believe that your MBA program will benefit from Louis as much as he will profit from a formal business school education. In other words, I believe that the investment will pay off handsomely for both your school and for him. I have no doubt that once he masters the business fundamentals, Louis DiDomenicantonio will definitely make waves in the game industry. If you have any questions regarding Louis or this recommendation, please contact me.

Sincerely,

To Whom It May Concern:

I have known Ruby Lopez-Ortiz for four and a half years as her direct supervisor at Ultima Technical. I am the Senior HR Consultant at the Chicago area corporate head-quarters, and I am pleased to recommend her for the FEMBA program at the University of Portsmouth.

I consider Ruby's most outstanding abilities to involve her technical expertise, her social skills, her creativity and her ability to handle pressure well. For example, she has a solid technical knowledge of HRIS software applications such as PeopleSoft, CSS Horizon, and Brio. Moreover, she has been tireless in utilizing those systems to enhance the administrative process with a strong focus on efficiency, timeliness and productivity. And she shares her technical expertise with others by providing systems training that is geared towards individual training needs after assessment analysis.

Ruby is a true team player who always makes herself available to provide sup-port to the HR team, which consists of about 25 staff members. In fact, I'm told that she gave her colleagues permission to call her for technical support while she was on her honeymoon, because she knew that the team was still adjusting to a set of novel ac-counting protocols that she had helped institute. Fortunately for us (and unfortunately for her), HR staffers did have to call her twice during her special vacation, but she walked them through the new protocols quite patiently and it definitely helped the team resolve the problem much faster than it would have otherwise been handled.

I have seen Ruby routinely make an effort to foster a stronger relationship be-tween Information Systems staff and HR staff as well as vendors such as our ADP clients. She has the ability to communicate effectively with all levels of the organiza-tion: end users, IT professionals, and HR professionals alike. Written evaluations of her HRIS training sessions often report that the workshops were fun and that Ruby made the information easier to retain by providing hands-on training sessions with personal and work-related examples.

An example of her creativity would be when she streamlined administration pro-cesses by creating workflow automation and visual workspace in the HR system. These creative features shortened the navigation time for the HR and payroll administrators during the data input process. They report that this change increased their productivity by 20%. I know that I can always count on Ruby to recommend several options for any problem-solving situation.

She is able to do all of this even during crunch time; I am thinking in particular about an HRIS system conversion that was mandated in our branch office about six months after she was hired. The upgrade itself was long overdue, but the data conversion, implementation and testing increased the workload of all HR personnel by about 30%. As project head, Ruby's personal workload increased by 70% for the month that it took to make the complete transition. She led different HR functional teams of ten people and delegated tasks in meeting deadlines and completing the system upgrade and conversion. Through it all, she set a brilliant example for the team by maintaining a remarkably positive outlook. When the position of HRIS Analyst opened up shortly afterwards, I did not hesitate to nominate her and support her fully for the promotion. Not only has Ruby achieved "superior" ratings on all her performance reviews to date, but she received an award for "Outstanding Employee" that year.

In my opinion, the FEMBA program is very appropriate at this time in Ruby's career, because she has indicated to me that she is interested in pursuing a position as Director of HR, for which an MBA degree is mandatory.

She will bring five years of work experience in the HR field to share with her MBA classmates; she is mature and responsible; and this is the perfect time for personal and professional development. I routinely recommend promising employees for business school, and in this context, Ruby is clearly in the top tier of that group.

Please contact me if I can be of any further service in discussing Ruby Lopez-Ortiz's skills and qualifications.

Sincerely,

Mayo Clinic
4273 Eleanor Way Portland, OR 78945

To Whom It May Concern:

I am pleased to give my heartiest recommendation for Carina Nguyen's application to the Family Medicine Residency. I worked closely with Ms. Nguyen during her four-week Family Medicine sub-internship at the Mayo Clinic, for which I am the attending physician. I have taught at the Mayo Clinic for twenty years; I serve as the clinical preceptor for three medical students each fall. It is my opinion that Ms. Nguyen performed at an exceptional level in acquiring the clinical competencies of Family Medicine and fulfilling her responsibilities as an integral team member of an inpatient medical service. She received a grade of "high pass," one earned by only 10% of the rotating medical students last year. I spent three half-days a week over the course of the internship directly observing Ms. Nguyen at Southern Cross Hospital. I base my evaluation of her skills on her participation and performance in morning reports, Grand Rounds and curriculum conferences, as well as the reports of the PGY-3 resident preceptor who supervised her day-to-day duties.

Ms. Nguyen, who already displayed a strong ability for clinical reasoning when she started the subinternship, further improved her ability to appraise, critically review and apply evidence from scientific studies and medical literature to her patients' health problems, as judging from her responses to assigned case protocols during our weekly conferences. In fact, I was pleased to see the level of her motivation to maximize her learning experience. She brought relevant references to curriculum conference on several occasions so that she could discuss them with me.

For the first two weeks, Ms. Nguyen handled a normal patient load of 3-5 patients. A set of extraordinary circumstances during the third week (i.e., the temporary closure of the Charles McFein Medical Center and subsequent increase of outpatient transfers) required us to ask the medical students to manage up to six patients for a few days. Ms. Nguyen acquitted herself well during this moment of great pressure. She even offered to take on another patient to help out a colleague who was clearly struggling with the workload; we could not approve this action, because subinterns are mandated to work with a maximum of six patients at a time, but I offer the anecdote as an illustration of her work ethic and her willingness to assume responsibility.

As it turned out, she had ample opportunity to apply her knowledge of the core curriculum and implement diagnostic and therapeutic plans. Ms. Nguyen was presented with the challenge of managing an unusually wide variety of illnesses that necessitated the entire range of routine clinical procedures, as well as her assistance on several advanced procedures (thoracentesis, paracentesis, and central line placement). Her technical skills were rated as very good. Exposure to this volume and diversity of clinical experience helped her fund of medical knowledge to develop rapidly.

The supervising PGY-3 resident who reviewed Ms. Nguyen's write-ups of patient histories, physical examinations, care plans, and daily problem-oriented progress briefings reported that all of his critiques were heeded and quickly applied; Ms. Nguyen even took the initiative to ask for constructive criticism. Not only did she excel in differential diagnoses, but she seemed to truly relish this line of investigatory and analytic thinking. Her ability to interpret diagnostic tests was exemplary. She demonstrated an advanced degree of independence and responsibility, and increasing confidence in her ability to develop and justify an appropriate differential and cohesive treatment plan as the subinternship progressed.

An integral part of any subinternship involves honing the medical student's interpersonal and communication skills. Ms. Nguyen also displayed commendable initiative in forming cordial and collegial relationships with professional colleagues and hospital personnel. She quickly won over her fellow subinterns, as well as the nursing and assistant staff, with her cheerful manner and generosity with her time; just as important, she was consistently attentive, accommodating, and respectful when interacting with colleagues and staff in a professional capacity. Lastly, she earned uniformly positive evaluations as a small group co-facilitator for sophomore students in the IPM-2 course.

As for her relations with patients, Ms. Nguyen was lauded by her resident preceptor for her thoroughness, thoughtfulness, and ability to communicate. Her ability to establish rapport quickly with pediatric patients was especially impressive. The professionalism that she carried into every interaction with patients, no matter how brief, did not go unnoticed. On one occasion, she had to enforce a patient's right to confidentiality when a female relative who was not authorized to receive the results of a sensitive medical test became agitated and belligerent; Ms. Nguyen firmly but kindly explained the hospital's position to the woman. The patient in question emailed us after being discharged, asking us to pass along his thanks to Ms. Nguyen for being so extraordinarily responsive to his needs in a very difficult situation.

To summarize, Ms. Carina Nguyen has been an outstanding Family Medicine subintern. Astute, thoughtful, and eager to learn, she pairs the detective skills of a diagnostician with the empathetic concern of a true caregiver and patient advocate. In both these respects, her level of maturity exceeds that of most at her level. She would reside very high on the NRMP rank list for our own Family Medicine training program; however, she has set her sights on a handful of residency programs in California. I feel confident in the knowledge that Ms. Nguyen will become one of those physicians who inspires deep trust and affection from patients, staff and colleagues alike. She has earned my wholehearted recommendation.

Sincerely,

UNIVERSITY OF CHICAGO
DEPARTMENT OF ELECTRICAL ENGINEERING AND COMPUTER SCIENCE

To Whom It May Concern:

I am delighted to recommend Sunil Roy for the UI Regents Postdoctoral Research Fellowship for the upcoming academic year. My recommendation is based upon my observations of Mr. Roy's scholarly activities and major teaching and administrative contributions to the University of Chicago Department of Electrical Engineering and Computer Science, of which I have served as the head for the past seven years.

Mr. Roy earned his Ph.D. from MIT in Electrical Engineering, during which time he also interacted considerably with the Department of Computer Science. He was hired two years ago as an Assistant Professor in the Electrical Engineering and Computer Science department at the University of Washington.

The dominant theme of Mr. Roy's research concerns the problems relating to the mining, analysis and summarization of multimedia data, especially as it pertains to applications for information extraction and utilization from large multimedia corpora. Most recently, he has focussed on the relationships between vision, audition, natural language and comprehension. His dissertation, "Statistical Pattern Discovery in Asynchronous Multi-Modal Streams," was supervised by Dr. Gene Smith. One of the dissertation chapters (reference #5) was revised for journal publication in ACM Multimedia and has been cited by several other scholars in the field.

Mr. Roy has established a reputation as one of the most promising young scholars in the field of multimedia mining. He has authored eight publications in peer-reviewed journals (five as principal author) and has presented findings of his research at multiple scientific meetings throughout North America, including the IEEE International Conference on Multimedia and Expo and the International Conference on Acoustic, Speech and Signal Processing. Mr. Roy has also contributed to two book chapters and published several technical reports.

The newest faculty member of our department has also fulfilled his teaching obligations with aplomb. Mr. Roy consistently receives outstanding reviews from students for his teaching ability. Mr. Roy has taken on primary advising duties for three graduate students as well as several undergraduates' independent research projects. His file contains letters from graduate students who express appreciation for Mr. Roy's thoughtful guidance and supervision.

During his fellowship year, Mr. Roy intends to further his investigations of multimedia mining and in particular, on the theoretical frameworks being used in multimodal analysis and multimedia information retrieval. His choice of University of Chicago as his sponsoring institution is motivated by the opportunity to avail himself of a research environment and mentoring opportunity that would be unavailable to him here at the University of Washington, where we currently do not have a senior faculty member working in this subfield of research.

In summary, Mr. Roy is a productive scholar who has utilized the tools of electrical engineering and computer science to investigate the theoretical and practical potential of multimedia mining. In addition to research contributions, he plays a leadership role by educational activities within the Department of Electrical Engineering and Computer Science. I enthusiastically endorse Mr. Roy's application for the UI Regents Postdoctoral Research Fellowship.

Sincerely,

P.S. The three most significant publications in Sunil Roy's curriculum vitae are reference numbers 2, 3 and 6.

University High School

1234 Any Street Chicago, Il 12345

To Whom It May Concern:

When Monica Satrapi told me that I was her first choice to write a letter supporting her application for the Liberty Foundation Scholarship, I have to say I wasn't surprised. As her AP Political Science teacher, I can certainly testify to the academic diligence that led her to score 5 (out of 5) on the rigorous AP test; however, both of us know what she really wanted me to write about: her fierce and unapologetic commitment to defending American values. As a committee evaluating candidates for qualified individuals who display the highest quality of understanding of the "Freedom Philosophy"—that is, how the United States Constitution impacts the individual's personal life—I can imagine that's where your interest lies as well.

At the end of the first week, Monica approached me after class to say that because English was not her first language, she wanted to get a head start on the first term paper. She said she had already completed the reading assignments through Week 3, and then asked me very seriously, "What topic should I write about, and what position would you like me to take on it?" Almost immediately, I saw the problem. Monica was a recent immigrant from an educational culture where the regurgitation of received wisdom is valued much higher than individual creativity. I told her that in order to excel on the AP test, she would need to show critical thinking, and that selecting her own topic, thesis and sources was a good place to start. I encouraged her to express her authentic reactions to the assigned readings in her dialectical journal entries—even if it meant challenging my point of view. As long as your arguments are supported by good evidence from reputable sources, I told her, you're free to argue what you like.

Monica clearly took my words to heart. Her first paper argued that the federal government should phase out Medicare. It was a minority view—politically conservative and decidedly not "politically correct"—but she supported her points with solid evidence. Her subsequent papers followed the same pattern—exhaustively researched, well-organized, and almost contrarian in their conservatism.

Then came the second phase of Monica's education in American freedoms: she learned to present these views in public. Halfway through the first semester, Monica took the opportunity to grumble about what she perceived as the liberal bias of her classmates—and asking me why I didn't refute them. "You're more than qualified to play devil's advocate yourself," I replied. Fifth period AP Political Science was never the same. Monica began to speak up in class, and she never failed to back up her opinion with a source. At first, her classmates were visibly bewildered; out of the blue, this previously silent girl was suddenly rebutting their comments, and asking them where their information had come from. When it became clear that she did not intend to return to silence, they started, one by one, to bring news printouts and clippings to class to serve as their own ammunition. The fact that she was at a linguistic disadvantage didn't deter her; it was obvious to all that she was borne aloft by the courage of her convictions. Almost singlehandedly, Monica managed to raise the level of discourse; she certainly made things more lively.

I can't remember how we all discovered that Monica was the editor of her church's youth newsletter, which was published in her own language, Farsi; likely, it was during a heated class argument about the racial profiling of air passengers when she let slip that her classmate's opinion was exactly the point of view that she refused to publish in her newsletter. When that classmate pointed out that Monica should extend to others the same freedom of speech she demanded for herself, it gave her pause, and she conceded the point. Later on, that classmate challenged Monica to print his views in her newsletter as an op-ed commentary. She clearly didn't like the idea. To my surprise, she eventually agreed to do so. Ironically, she ended up having to translate her classmate's short essay into Farsi. Even more ironically, she told me later with grim humor, the piece kicked up a mild flurry in the church community and she had found herself defending free speech principles to her parents. Personally, I can't think of a better example of the Constitution influencing a student's personal growth.

Monica doesn't just believe in freedom of speech—she lives it out loud. I suspect that moving to the United States, where she could express herself to her heart's content, was the best thing to ever happen to her. She said to me once: "If I hadn't moved here, I think I might have exploded from holding all these ideas in." She was made for an American classroom; and I don't think it's going too far to say that her immigrant zeal for her constitutional right to dissent and self-expression shamed her native-born classmates—and then inspired them to rethink and refine their own arguments. I certainly don't agree with all of her views. But I can only hope that my future classes will bring me other Monica Satrapis. Students who believe this passionately in their views—and more importantly, who uphold the principles of liberty that allow unpopular views to be expressed—deserve to be recognized. I hope you do so by granting Ms. Satrapi the Liberty Foundation Scholarship. She has my strongest recommendation.

Please let me know if you need me to provide any more information to support her application.

Sincerely,

CAMP ASPIRE

To Whom It May Concern:

     As someone who has known Carlotta Williams for more than six years, I am so terribly pleased to have the chance to write a letter of recommendation for her. I understand that the Gates Millennium Scholarship selection committee is seeking well-deserving students who have demonstrated strong leadership in community service activities, as well as academic excellence. Because I serve as Head Counselor of Camp Aspire, a residential summer camp for low-income youth, I feel well-qualified to comment on Carlotta's natural leadership abilities.

     Carlotta, a straight-A student, has been one of our finest Counselors-in-Training (a.k.a CIT) at Camp Aspire for the past two years. She is a warm, generous girl with a sensible head on her shoulders; not only can she sense right away when somebody is floundering and needs help, but she steps up with a big smile and volunteers her assistance without being prompted. Helping others really is second nature for her.

     Carlotta is very familiar with Camp Aspire; before working as a CIT, she was a camper here herself for three years. Over the years, I have found out that Carlotta comes from a large clan. She is the eldest of five children, and because she was the firstborn, she had to take on a lot of caregiving responsibility for her siblings. Obviously that's where she got to be so good at managing young children – being able to anticipate their needs and distract them from their fears.

     My favorite example of her leadership skills involves a nature walk. For many of these inner city kids, this guided introduction to the mountain forest ecosystem is their first exposure to nature; Carlotta herself loved it so much. Every year, she came back knowing more scientific plant names because she had looked them up before she came to camp. When she became a CIT, you could tell how much she enjoyed sharing her botanical knowledge with the campers.

     This year, Carlotta was the CIT for the Panda Gang, a cluster of nine-year-old girls. As they headed out on the nature walk, a camper named Janie tripped and skinned her knee; Carlotta was there in a flash with the first aid kit and to soothe Janie's tears; in the midst of the hubbub, somebody noticed that another camper had wandered off. Without missing a beat, Carlotta recruited the nearest Panda and gave her clear, careful instructions about taking over with applying pressure to the bandage on Janie's knee. Then she quieted the rest of the group and asked them to yell loudly in unison: "SUZY! WHERE ARE YOU! COME BACK TOWARDS US!" Carlotta stood up and began to search the surrounding area—without ever letting the group out of her sight.

Within three minutes, Suzy was found and returned to the fold, and the whole group was given a stern but kind lecture about the dangers of wandering off on their own. Carlotta gave Janie a piggy-back ride back to the cabin—where the Panda Gang promptly told the rest of us what had just happened.

Not only is she level-headed in a crisis, but Carlotta is an excellent role model, and she knows how to motivate a team. At the same time, she knows what's most important. Every summer, Camp Aspire always ends with the Aspiration Olympics, which pits teams of campers against each other in a series of competitions that takes place over four days. How did Carlotta keep her Green Team motivated when they were dead last in the standings for the first two full days? She must have given some amazing pep talks, because they managed an amazing comeback on the last day. For a while, it looked like they might win the whole thing, but they ended up second place when they lost the final event, the Tug of War. In my experience, the runner-up team is usually in tears for the rest of the day—these games bring out a competitive spirit in campers that is really quite intense. But this year, the Green Team campers walked up in a big group to the winning Red Team to shake hands. That gesture of sportsmanship had Carlotta's fingerprints all over it.

On the last day of camp, she was very emotional, as it probably hit her that she would not be returning to Camp Aspire next summer. It must have felt like the end of an era for her, but I know that she'll make a difference in so many other lives when she goes to college and gets involved in clubs and organizations there. This is just the beginning!

Carlotta Williams is exactly the kind of student that your Gates Millennium Scholarship is designed to help. She would only be the second person in her immediate family to attend college, and I can assure you that she is so excited about the prospect of studying Biology. She wants to be a doctor, and your generous scholarship will help make it happen. To reiterate, I am so proud of Carlotta for her ambition and her accomplishments, and this terrific young lady has my highest recommendation.

Sincerely,

Ralston College 4345 Campus Road Boston, MA 01245

To Whom It May Concern:

It is a privilege for me to nominate Seth Pella for the Leadership Fellows program. In my eight years of teaching at Ralston College, only once have I taught a student with equivalent leadership potential; that was Ulrich Benz in 1999, whom I also nominated—successfully—for the Leadership Fellows program, and who, as you well know, is now serving as a State Assemblyman.

Although I met Mr. Pella for the first time when he enrolled in my course, "New Media Technologies," his reputation preceded him. Last year, he was one of the activist leaders behind a series of rallies protesting a controversial proposed exhibit of Native American mummies at the Borcher Museum, which is affiliated with our university. During these protests, Mr. Pella was quoted in the campus newspaper as saying: "Students should be responsible for their own education. We can't just expect teachers to hand us information." I photocopied the article, circled that quote with a highlighter, and taped it to my office door. I couldn't have expressed it better myself—that young people learn best when they are motivated to dig for knowledge on their own—and I hoped that students waiting their turn for office hours would get the message.

I first became aware that this astute young man was enrolled in my course when my teaching assistant began telling me about a particular student whose enthusiasm for dialogue outstripped anything she'd ever experienced, either as an instructor or a student. According to my TA, this Mr. Pella not only posed smart questions that clearly showed a critical grasp of the readings, but unusually for a college student, he often addressed these questions in a collegial way to his classmates, soliciting their opinion and citing their previous responses. In effect, he was actively helping to lead and guide the discussion—practically doing the TA's work for her. Not surprisingly, he had become very popular with the other students.

Two weeks into the semester, Mr. Pella requested a transfer into my discussion section because of a scheduling conflict. This gave me—as well as his new set of classmates—the chance to experience his gregarious classroom style and natural leadership ability. I came to conclude that Mr. Pella's friendliness is irrepressible and unmistakably sincere. He is deeply interested in other people and their opinions, and listens intently. He brought such a sociable, welcoming energy that even the shyest felt safe to speak up. As concerns his writing skills, I found Mr. Pella's papers to be well-researched and cogently argued. And almost invariably, his thesis was informed by an intriguing avenue of conversation or set of ideas that he had helped elicit from his classmates. It is a talent to be able to awaken curiosity in others; Mr. Pella used that gift to generate discussion, and whenever provocative intellectual connections were made, he took them seriously as points to investigate further.

I will conclude with an anecdote about the admirable integrity and responsibility that I see in this future leader. In March, Mr. Pella invited me to attend the final rally at the museum, where he would be delivering a speech; anticipation was high because local media were scheduled to cover the event. When I showed up at the appointed time, however, I saw no signs of an assembly. Later that day, Mr. Pella emailed me to explain that he had made the painful decision to cancel the rally at the last minute because of rumors that a fringe group of protesters were planning to deface the museum's signage during the event. As he told me later, although many of his supporters faulted him for squandering a priceless public relations opportunity, he had no regrets about following his conscience. In fact, the gesture may have been instrumental in thawing the opposition's recalcitrance. The next day, after weeks of refusing to meet with the protesters, the museum administration extended a quiet invitation; the ensuing talks have led to an unprecedented compromise regarding the number of artifacts to be displayed and the language that will be used to describe them.

This incident only confirmed for me that Mr. Pella's priorities as a leader and activist are exactly right. Although he was passionate for justice, he was not willing to tolerate anarchistic acts, no matter how minor. He demonstrated respect for the process, even when it placed him at a disadvantage.

Having had the distinct pleasure of teaching Seth Pella (or perhaps I should say, participating in the education he was creating for himself), I offer my heartiest endorsement of his candidacy for the Leadership Fellows program. I believe he will throw himself into the training, and take full advantage of all its resources. I expect to hear much more about Seth Pella in years to come. Whatever career he chooses for himself, he will be an ambassador—in the true sense of the word—who brings people together and urges them to do their best while never compromising their core values. Surely this fits the program's mission statement to a tee?

If I may offer further information about this nominee, please do not hesitate to contact me.

Sincerely,

CALIFORNIA
STATE
UNIVERSITY

To Whom It May Concern:

As the faculty sponsor for Scott Yamanaka's research, I am writing in support of his Undergraduate Research Opportunities Program grant application; I have agreed to serve as his research mentor and supervise his study measuring the effect of meditation on impulse control.

If Mr. Yamanaka's name seems familiar to the Advisory Board, it is because he is a past recipient of UROP funding; two years ago, he was a co-applicant for a group research project under Dr. Joely Martinsen's supervision ("Anxiety and Self-Confidence in Relation to Individual and Team Sports"). I am told that the poster was extremely well-received. Considering Mr. Yamanaka's productive history with UROP, I ask that you approve the individual project proposal that he is submitting this year under my sponsorship.

Project
Mr. Yamanaka proposes to empirically demonstrate the relationship between short-term meditative practice and impulsivity, as measured by the Porteus Maze Test. The study will enroll 40 participants: 20 who will be trained in and practice Zen meditation for a period of 30 minutes every day for eight weeks, and a control group of 20 who will be asked to merely sit quietly for the same amount of time. Participants will be assessed for impulse control at the beginning and at the end of the two-month study. It is hypothesized that the meditating group will score higher than their baseline and significantly higher than the control group at the final testing.

Significance
The effect of meditation on other cognitive functions, such as academic performance and attention regulation, has been researched, but this would be, to my knowledge, the first study to specifically study the effect of meditation on impulse control. Low levels of impulse control have been linked to a range of psychological disorders (ADHD, pathological gambling, kleptomania, and violent psychopathy), and addictive behaviors (drug, nicotine, and alcohol use). A direct correlation between meditation practice and improved measures of impulse control would add to the body of empirical data on the benefits of meditation as a therapy for compulsive behavior disorders and addictions.

Budget
The proposed project is decidedly low-tech; most of the requested funds would be allocated to compensating the human subjects for their time. I believe the overall request for $1200 to be not unreasonable for a study of this size.

Mr. Yamanaka sought me out as a faculty sponsor on his own initiative. He had taken my course, Abnormal Psychology, last summer. However, when he approached me to request my assistance with his proposed study, I did not know him. He presented me with a short précis sketching out the project design and explained that his project seemed to dovetail with my research interests in anxiety disorders and cognitive behavioral therapy. Mr. Yamanaka also mentioned that his intellectual curiosity on this topic was personally motivated. Several of his young cousins and nephews have been diagnosed with ADHD. Recently, he happened upon an article positing that children with attention deficit disorders are considered more susceptible to adult drug addiction, and he realized that his siblings' children were vulnerable. He channeled his concern into informal research on the causes and treatments of ADHD and became intrigued by non-pharmacological therapies of same.

I found his hypothesis intriguing. Before I agreed to serve as his research mentor, however, I consulted the graduate student instructor who had graded his papers in Abnormal Psychology, and reviewed his writing assignments and exams myself. Mr. Yamanaka also provided me with a copy of the "Anxiety and Self-Confidence in Relation to Individual and Team Sports" paper. After perusing the abstract and data analysis, I was satisfied that Mr. Yamanaka had sufficient grounding in social science research methodology. Over the past two months, I have worked closely with him, first to undertake a more systematic review of the literature on these topics, and subsequently to flesh out his hypothesis and project design. Based on my observation of his work ethic, critical thinking, and analytical skills, I believe that Mr. Yamanaka is more than capable of carrying out the project as described in his proposal.

With or without UROP funding, Mr. Yamanaka will be conducting this research under my supervision as an independent study project (he has enrolled in Psychology 199), because his current part-time status renders him ineligible to enroll officially in the Psychology Departmental Honors Thesis program. He and I agreed that I would hold him to the same high standards of an honors thesis, both in terms of length and quality.

Mr. Yamanaka is prepared to spend two months conducting this study, and one additional month analyzing the data and writing up the results. To support his research, I have offered to make my laboratory space available to him. I have also budgeted time to meet with him on a weekly basis to review and give feedback on his progress reports; to supervise the administration of the Porteus Maze Tests to the research subjects; to vet his statistical analysis; and to advise on possible venues for presentation and publication when the study is complete. As noted earlier, a significant portion of the proposed funding would compensate the human subjects for their time; absent UROP funding, I am prepared to assist Mr. Yamanaka's recruitment efforts by offering nominal extra credit to Psychology undergraduate students as an incentive to participate in the research study.

I will conclude by reviewing my own qualifications for serving as a faculty mentor. In addition to my normal teaching load, I am currently supervising four other undergraduate students with their research; one of those is a Psychology Departmental Honors Thesis; the others are independent study projects. In the past six years, I have been a UROP Faculty Research Mentor for three other students, all of whom have gone on to pursue graduate-level research in Psychology. Anand Gill was published as a second author in the American Journal of Family Therapy and was later accepted into the highly-ranked Ph.D program at Duke University; Margaret Scofield is currently deciding between attending the University of Chicago and Northwestern; and Dean Flanders has a publication pending in Applied Cognitive Psychology. In my opinion, Scott Yamanaka compares very favorably to those other UROP fundees, both in terms of his general academic potential for research and the tenor of this project. I believe that funding his proposal would be a wise investment on the part of the UROP.

Sincerely,

Coastline College

To Whom It May Concern:

I gladly write this letter of recommendation for Mr. Gary Vanderveer, who is applying for the Summer Research Institute at Johns Hopkins. I have supervised him as a student researcher in my laboratory for the past year, though our acquaintance precedes that by another year. In that time, I have had the unique pleasure of witnessing a bright young student discover and embrace a latent scientific vocation.

I am a full professor of molecular biology and have taught for 24 years at Coastline College; I received my Ph.D. from Rutgers University in 1978 and did post-doctoral work at Indiana University. My lab, which employs four graduate students, and five undergraduates, has as its primary research focus the basic scientific processes of mitochondrial biogenesis, mitochondrial protein import, and regulation of gene expression in yeast. I serve on the editorial board of the Journal of Molecular Biology, and I have served as faculty textbook consultant for several academic publishers. Of the two dozen or so students that I have recommended in the past for NSF-sponsored REU programs, eleven have gone on to pursue doctoral level work in biology. I believe Mr. Vanderveer will make it a lucky dozen.

It seems to be the case that when Mr. Vanderveer first applied for the work-study position of laboratory assistant as a sophomore, he had no scientific ambitions beyond autoclaving pipettes and beakers, much less plans to use this position as a launchpad for a research career. For one thing, he was an Anthropology major. When I asked his reasons for applying to work in my lab, he replied that he was considering doing a field study of a biological research lab for his Anthropology honors program thesis project. It was an unusual request, but because he appeared well-spoken and responsible—not to mention amply qualified to wash glassware and prepare solutions, reagents and media—I hired him.

Over the course of the year, his interest in the culture of research environments gradually shifted to fascination with the science itself; members of my group told me that Mr. Vanderveer's questions about the research techniques, protocols and objectives were becoming increasingly sophisticated. In fact, of his own initiative, this young man sought out and read several of our lab's published articles, essentially doing the "homework" that I usually assign my undergraduate researchers before I allow them to start working on any projects. Although Mr. Vandeveer had a basic scientific grounding from his high school AP Biology experience, he was—understandably—out of his depth with many of the journal articles; he took every opportunity to ask for clarification of the procedures and concepts that he was unfamiliar with. By Spring Quarter, he had enrolled in a couple of core Biology courses, in part to fulfill university breadth requirements, but also because he wanted to upgrade the quality of his participation in the lab. I told Mr. Vanderveer that if he managed a B+ or better in Biochemistry as well as a summer session Genetics course, he would be welcome in my lab as a student researcher. Although I generally try to reserve positions in my lab for undergraduates with an expressed interest in pursuing a medical or research career, I rarely turn down applicants whom I believe have the intellectual capacity and work ethic to make a valuable contribution to our projects.

For the past year, Mr. Vanderveer has done just that. His primary duties were to assist my doctoral candidates in defining the regulatory elements that control the expression of regulated nuclear genes, utilizing the yeast Saccharomyces cerevisiae. Over time, he proved proficient enough that I placed him in charge of isolating DNA samples, a complex and involved process that has tested many a fledgling researcher's dexterity and patience. His performance confirmed that laboratory research suits Mr. Vanderveer's highly perceptive and methodical temperament and aptitude for analytical thinking. He continued to enroll in Biology and Chemistry courses, and often asked about research applications based on the content in those classes. Our laboratory's recent work has focused on two aspects of the complex problem of mitochondrial biogenesis. We have been trying to define the regulatory elements that control the expression of a pair of inversely regulated genes, particularly COX5a and COX5b. Despite his non-science background—or perhaps because of it—Mr. Vanderveer offered intriguing, out-of-the-box insights.

He also works very hard. Mr. Vanderveer has repeatedly demonstrated his commitment to his research responsibilities by staying after hours to finish autoclaving cultures. It is my understanding that his exceptional diligence is motivated by the feeling that he has to make up for starting "late" in Biology.

Over the course of my career, I have employed a handful of researchers who were not explicitly committed to a research career and for whom therefore I could do very little from a mentoring standpoint. You can imagine that I was initially a little skeptical about Mr. Vanderveer; as with these others, his early enthusiasm for lab work might prove to be a kind of short-lived infatuation. And yet somehow it did not come as a complete surprise when Mr. Vanderveer told me that he had declared a second major in Biology. I see that he is extremely motivated to make the most of his remaining undergraduate years, and I find his dedication to my lab and our projects very gratifying. It is not lost on me that the decision to double major will necessitate that he defer his graduation for two or three quarters. I do not think he is extending his college career merely to fulfill his intellectual curiosity; when I asked if he were considering graduate work in Biology, he said he couldn't promise anything just yet. However, just last week he scheduled a meeting to ask me about opportunities to present his findings at undergraduate conferences and symposia. We have already discussed the individual research project he'll be working on next fall, and the publication opportunities to which it might lead.

In short, I believe that you can help me encourage a promising young researcher and nurture his career by accepting Mr. Vanderveer for your REU. He will bring serious purpose, analytical rigor, and a thirst for learning to any lab that takes him. I have specifically advised him to apply to programs that offer research infrastructure and opportunities unavailable to him here at Alabama State. Because he has essentially indicated that he is seriously considering a career in academic research, I believe that it is important for him to experience research at a major university, such as Johns Hopkins. I have no doubt that the experience will enhance his technical skills, augment his scientific knowledge, and positively influence his career decisions.

If you have any further questions, please feel free to contact me.

Sincerely,

SpeakEasy Communications

473 Business Road, Suite 240 St. Paul, MN
(595) 555-5460

To Whom It May Concern:

It gives me enormous pleasure to support Imogene Carey's application to the Congress-Bundestag Youth Exchange for Young Professionals scholarship program. Having supervised her work for the past eighteen months, I feel highly qualified to speak on her potential to succeed in a program that emphasizes diplomacy, learning, and networking—and which will culminate in a business internship. I run a company called SpeakEasy Communications, which offers presentation skills training for all occasions. As my administrative assistant, Imogene is mainly responsible for coordinating our schedule of public speaking and interview coaching courses. I understand that the CBYX for Young Professionals program's ideal applicant is a skillful communicator, exhibits flexibility and diplomacy, and possesses clear career goals. Allow me to address each of these points briefly in regards to Imogene Carey.

Communication

Given my line of business, I consider myself an excellent judge of communication skills; I have been sufficiently impressed by Imogene's abilities in this respect that I recently asked her to develop and lead her own workshop for our pre-medical clients. Many of these students experience strong anxiety about the prospect of discussing current events at their admissions interviews. Knowing that Imogene had majored in International Relations, I saw an opportunity to leverage another one of her skill sets to provide more value to our clients. I tasked her with developing a workshop that would prepare our clients and prospects to speak on current events. Within a week, she put together a seminar on how to understand and discuss domestic and international events and trends, as well as hot-button topics in health care. I would rate Imogene's public speaking skills as well above average. Her style is confident, friendly, and informed. She takes real joy in sharing her knowledge—and in making sure that everybody fully understands the content. Many of the participants have told me that they enjoyed the workshop tremendously.

Flexibility

My preferred management style with employees is to describe my vision of a project and give them the latitude to figure out what resources they need to complete the project. Imogene excels at working independently to assess and prioritize the assignments. If I ask her to quickly learn a new software application or train another employee in a certain procedure, coordinate the logistics of my recent national speaking tour or develop a monthly newsletter that is sent out to nearly 8,500 subscribers, I can depend on her to complete her assignments on time. My schedule is very tight, and I consider micromanaging to be a waste of my time. Imogene intuited this very early on, and adapted to fit my style. At the same time, she is unembarrassed to ask for assistance when doing so will help her perform her job more efficiently. Her commitment is to the job, not her ego. I feel good knowing that once I clarify a technical process or explain a coaching concept to Imogene, the information is assimilated, shaped into a problem-solving tool, and put to use right away.

Diplomacy

Of course, the willingness to accommodate others is merely a nice gesture unless one is prepared or equipped to truly be of service. I am reminded of a recent business trip to Mexico City, where Imogene put her linguistic and cultural expertise to skillful use as my interpreter and guide. Diplomacy goes far beyond speaking with discretion; in my opinion, it's impossible unless you first establish a relationship of trust and rapport. Many of the people we met with in Mexico were prepared to converse with us in English, but Imogene would instinctively put them at ease by addressing them in Spanish and giving them the opportunity to negotiate in their native tongue. In a very real sense, Imogene Carey was my calling card to doing business in Mexico.

Flexibility in the service of diplomacy is quite a virtue. Part of that is taking the time to listen and learn what people value. When we first sat down with one immigration lawyer to pitch him on co-sponsoring an ambitious seminar series on U.S. immigration and employment interview coaching, the man seemed skeptical and wary; he was clearly assessing us. As she translated for me, Imogene noticed that his accent marked him as being from the south of Mexico. Without missing a single beat, she discreetly scribbled a note to me that I should ask him about his background. I did, and as he told me about his hometown in the Yucatan, he visibly relaxed. Finally, the lawyer said to me, "The next time you come to Mexico, we will do business the Mexican way—over a tequila lunch." That was when we knew he had decided that we were worth negotiating with. Without Imogene there to broker the relationship, I doubt that I could have achieved such a successful result.

By combining intangible charm and concrete preparation, Imogene Carey makes it easy for other people to take small risks that can pay off in a big way. My company's customer service training is predicated on a very similar concept: by emphasizing that both parties all have something to gain by entertaining new possibilities, we open the door to finding out what other people truly need and whether we can work with them. Clearly, Imogene has internalized this idea deeply.

Career Goals

Imogene has often spoken to me of her ambition to work in international marketing. You could say that she's been preparing for it her entire life—long before she chose to major in International Relations or study abroad in Chile. First of all, thanks to her family ties to South America and Europe, she has traveled a lot since she was very young. I think this facilitated her understanding that the world is both bigger and smaller than it appears—cultures can differ widely, hence ambassadors are important; people's needs are universal, therefore it's possible to find common ground. Growing up embodying several cultures—Jewish, Latina, and American—has made her broadminded instead of insular; I believe that being able to move between cultures with relative ease has motivated her to reach out to others who would like to experience something new. It allows her to see possibilities and tell people: "You may not see a way across, but I assure you that there is a bridge. Let's cross it together."

Outside of everything I have already mentioned, Imogene is really a pleasure to be around. Her sense of humor is warm, mischievous, good-natured. She thrives on hard work and honest accomplishment. I believe she is motivated by the desire to see how far her skills will take her. In short, I couldn't be prouder of the ownership she has taken of her role at SpeakEasy, and I'm thrilled to have given her the space to test her wings. It is so obvious to me that Imogene is on the cusp of a promising career which will allow her to combine her cross-cultural competence and passion for business. Because she is committed to that goal, I can assure you that she will maximize the educational and networking opportunities provided by the CBYX for Young Professionals program. I recommend her for your program without reservation.

Please don't hesitate to contact me if you require more information.

Sincerely,

HENRY JONES
1234 SOUTH STREET
ANYTOWN, CA 90010
(818)555-1234

To Whom It May Concern:

I am writing this letter to assure you that Melanie Lalas will be an excellent worker. Although she is just 15 years old, she is up to the challenge of performing the job duties that you require of her. I have known her for more than a year. She was recommended to me by a fellow parent from the KidzKlub Day Care center when I was looking for a new babysitter to watch my two boys (ages 5 and 7) on occasional evenings.

Melanie impressed me from the start with her professionalism. First of all, Melanie exhibited a very pleasant, courteous manner that differentiates her from most teenagers that I interact with nowadays. And one of the first things she did—without being asked—was to show me her CPR/First Aid certification card. She also volunteered a list of strategies that she said she usually used with young kids, asking if we approved. We did indeed. The only thing we added was that we had a strict no-TV policy with our children. Melanie never deviated from it. This was important to us, since our previous babysitter had violated our wishes on this issue.

Our boys, Trevor and Lincoln, liked Melanie so much that they began asking when she would come back to play with them. My wife and I came to trust her so much that we even asked her to drop by and water our plants while we were on a two-week vacation. We came back to find our plants thriving and the mail sorted by date and recipient. And if I'm not mistaken, the living room was neater than when we had left it.

If the job position that you're seeking to fill requires patience, Melanie has got it. Believe me, anybody who can handle a rambunctious 5-year-old and a smart-alecky 7-year-old without resorting to using television as a pacifier is someone who has stamina and great problem-solving skills.

I also know that Melanie was recently elected treasurer of her sophomore class. That is a position of responsibility that I think speaks not only to her ability to stay organized, but also to the social skills that enabled her to win the votes of her peers.

She is bright, personable, and takes responsibility seriously. Most important, she is constantly looking to improve herself. She learns very quickly. I have myself happily referred Melanie to two other parents, and both of whom have thanked me for introducing them to such a reliable and conscientious babysitter. Melanie may be starting off in an entry-level position, but I predict that within a few months her excellent performance and work ethic will have you looking for ways to promote her to a position of greater responsibility. I simply can't say enough good things about her.

Sincerely,

To Whom It May Concern:

This letter of reference is sent on behalf of Mihaly Leoben, who worked in my employ for the past two years. I am the owner of Haven Studios, a high-end photographic and digital studio space which regularly hosts corporate events, private parties, fashion shows, art exhibitions, product launches, and television and film shoots. On a daily basis, Mr. Leoben is responsible for marketing and strategic outreach operations for Haven. He plays an integral role in maintaining and increasing our prospect base, and finding new markets.

I would describe Mihaly Leoben as a young man with enormous potential, and I can attest to his maturity. Although only 24 when we hired him for the Special Events Marketing Coordinator position, he had a precocious sense of creativity and tenacity that impressed me. I have been pleased to observe those traits continue to mature and deepen. And I have no qualms about relating an anecdote in which Mihaly's out-of-the-box thinking persuaded me to overrule my previous assumptions.

In short, I give Mihaly credit for discovering a new market niche for our studio, namely, weekend breakfast/brunch galas for foreign students. He championed the idea—and then gestated it, nurtured it, and carried it to term. In fact, he brought up the idea when I first interviewed him for this position. He asked me about Haven's capacity for hosting morning events on weekdays, and if I had any plans to expand that capacity. "Nothing would make me happier," I replied, "but it's not practical at this time." A few years ago I had determined that there was not enough interest in weekday catered breakfast/brunch events of the type we could offer; I had made an executive decision to focus on afternoon and evening events. I made it clear that establishing a regular slate of morning events was simply not a priority. My answer, however, didn't satisfy Mihaly. He felt passionately that we were underutilizing our event space and calendar. After a few weeks of brainstorming and research, he came up with a suggestion that was both ingenious and fortuitous. Ingenious, because it capitalized on our studio's "one-stop shop" capability. Fortuitous, because he picked up the idea from a casual comment made by his brother.

To give a little background: With Seattle's proximity to the Pacific Rim countries as well as Latin America, one of our city's fastest growing industries is English as a Second Language (ESL) education. The downtown core is studded with private language schools that serve foreign students who have ventured abroad to learn English in an immersion and homestay environment. Mihaly, whose brother works as the director of one such school, told me that in order to compete in a crowded field, many schools are offering their students increasingly lavish graduation lunches and hiring a professional photographer to shoot commemorative "prom-style" portraits. "Wouldn't Haven be ideal for combining the two, with our in-house catering service and on-site photographic equipment and facilities?" he asked. All we had to do was convince ESL directors that their students would enjoy celebrating their graduation a little earlier in the day, with an "All-American brunch" banquet.

Mihaly took the initiative to do the research and reach out to potential business partners. In March, he used a Power Point presentation to officially pitch me on the market potential and the cost-benefit of hiring additional staff to cover morning shifts beyond our current weekend schedule. I am happy to take business risks if I feel that the market research supports the possibility of a good return, and Mihaly's data were persuasive enough. For example, he pointed out that these breakfast brunches could offer not be highly seasonal because ESL schools offer language courses of varying lengths and therefore graduate classes throughout the year. Secondly, they only hold classes and "field trips" on weekdays, and therefore these special breakfasts would not cut into our established weekend brunch business. Mihaly also gave valuable input when we designed a series of customized priced packages and menus.

We held our first ESL brunch banquet eight months ago; since then we have hosted 18 similar events—12 bookings in the last three months alone. We have established relationships with 10 Seattle-area language schools so far, and are building a unique reputation for this all-inclusive food-and-photography package. Client satisfaction has been very high, and the growth potential for this offering looks quite positive.

Mihaly's tenacity on this issue paid dividends. He has demonstrated to me that he is willing to go to bat for ideas that he believes in strongly enough. Just as important, he understands how necessary it is to lay the groundwork so that others can feel good about taking a risk.

By asking certain questions ("Why have we never ventured into this new market before? What would happen if we tried?"), Mihaly Leoben demonstrated a sense of initiative and enterprising curiosity that proved stronger than my initial demurrals. He had the gumption to think big—and the work ethic to carry out those big plans. He was driven to make the experiment, which is why I fully understand and support his decision to pursue fresh professional challenges. I highly recommend Mr. Leoben for any marketing position that you are considering him for.

Sincerely,

To Whom It May Concern:

This is written in response to your request for a reference for Nueng Khounpaseuth that discusses her work ethic and performance. I am the proprietor of Toussaint, a Caribbean-themed casual dining restaurant that does 300-400 covers a night; I hired Ms. Khounpaseuth four years ago, and it was one of the best staffing decisions I ever made. She came to us with substantial experience in both heart-of-the-house and back-of-the-house operations, having previously worked as a station cook, sous chef and expediter. At Toussaint, she worked Kitchen Manager duties (handling inventory and purchasing, supervising the prep kitchen staff) during the day, and worked as our expediter during dinner service. For four years, she has been utterly dependable—and I mean that as high praise. I could depend on her to keep the kitchen clean, stocked, and efficient. I could depend on her commitment to high standards. I could even depend on her to surprise me all over again with an ingenious cost-cutting measure or an announcement that she'd found a better supplier for a certain food item.

As a result of profitability and efficiency improvements initiated by Ms. Khounpaseuth, our San Antonio store has benefited from a cost savings of 8% and a rise in revenue per guest of over 12%, resulting in an increase of profits in excess of 15% during her tenure.

Her communication skills are first-rate, and her leadership style is plain-spoken. In other letters of reference, that would be a euphemism for tactless and short-tempered, but I mean it exactly like it sounds. She's tough but fair; she lays out all her expectations up front; if somebody fails to perform, she immediately communicates not only her dissatisfaction but how they can make things right. No grudges, no name-calling, definitely no screaming. Ms. Khounpaseuth really looks out for her crew in the kitchen; they know that she'll take their side if they have a legitimate grievance. She expects them to do their best. Because they see her giving 110% every-day—they're inclined to push themselves harder.

She proved her value a thousand times a week, but if I had to choose one incident, it would be this: during a heat wave last summer, our grill cook actually passed out on line due to the heat and stress. Within thirty seconds, Ms. Khounpaseuth saw him wobbling, yelled for somebody to attend to him, stepped up to the grill, plated five orders and started another five. (Days like these remind us why we demand that our Kitchen Managers be able to perform all kitchen positions).

In total, she has recruited and trained eight kitchen staff (all good hires). When we opened our Austin store, I recommended that Ms. Khounpaseuth spend a day there to train the kitchen manager in her best practices. Based on her food and beverage knowledge, she also helped develop two new appetizers (Coconut-Toasted Calamari, Jerked Scallops Roti) and a drink (the Guavatini) that have been adopted at all of our locations.

I'm sure you can appreciate how difficult it is to find a competent kitchen manager, much less a great one. Given all my fulsome praise, you may be wondering why Ms. Khounpaseuth came to find herself looking for a new job—or, if you've already asked her, you may want me to independently confirm her story. I assure you that she did not leave Toussaint because we were in any way dissatisfied with her performance. A while ago, she bought a house upstate, which doubled the length of her commute. She tried the arrangement out for two months, but finally decided that the drive time had become unacceptable. I offered her several financial incentives to stay, but she was resolved to find a job closer to home. If you have received her application, your restaurant lies within her acceptable driving radius. Lucky you.

Don't make the mistake of passing on Ms. Khounpaseuth. She'll organize your kitchen, whip your kitchen crew into shape and win their loyalty, identify and rectify wasteful practices, and keep the kitchen service humming, night after night. She'll bring tough-minded purchasing practices that will in all likelihood help you cut costs. If you ask, she'll offer valuable insights in shaping the menu to utilize seasonal foods. She's a keeper.

Sincerely,

Kappen Occupational Health
Medical Group

To Whom It May Concern:

I am responding to your request for a letter of recommendation for Donal Mulkerrin. He has worked at Kappen Occupational Health Medical Group for the last four years, progressing rapidly from sales representative to manager. Kappen is the second largest occupational health provider in the Pacific Northwest. We offer a full range of wellness and prevention, physical therapy, injury care, and drug testing services to help employers maintain a healthy workforce.

Before I transferred to another regional office, Mr. Mulkerrin worked under my direct supervision for a little over two years, between October 200x and January 200x. During that period, I watched him develop from a junior sales trainee—responsible for securing contracts and marketing our clinic for Workers Compensation and Urgent Care Services—into a highly effective District Sales Manager. In the latter position, his purview expanded to focus on prospecting markets, bringing in new corporate accounts, as well as maintaining and up-selling to our current client base, not to mention training and supervising a sales staff of eight. When I was consulted about my replacement as District Sales Manager, Donal was my top choice despite having slightly less seniority than another candidate. His fantastic performance in the position has more than validated my recommendation for his promotion.

With his take-charge personality and his agile intelligence, Mr. Mulkerrin is someone whom I could depend on to immediately grasp the challenges of a new market or account, and then to present me with a strategic plan of how to get it done. During his two years as a Sales Representative, he often exceeded his monthly sales targets; as District Manager, he successfully met the regimented quarterly sales targets, which speaks volumes about the way he was able to motivate his team to perform to expectations. In his first fiscal year as manager, he achieved 112.5% of plan; in his second year, it was 130%.

Personally, I think his success in workers compensation/industrial medicine sales is directly related to the fact that he used to be a Physician Assistant himself. The stories that he can tell about diagnosing illnesses or setting broken bones give him extra credibility with prospective clients. Besides that, I've always suspected that his medical training taught him how to cut out all the extraneous information and zone in on what was important, such as diagnosing the main obstacle when a prospect proved especially difficult to close. Of course, his success could just as easily be due to the fact that Donal Mulkerrin possesses ambition and resourcefulness in spades. He is a natural communicator, always ready with a joke or an anecdote. He has also been especially successful with getting new business through referrals, based on the cordial relationships that he builds and maintains with relevant managers at our client companies.

To say that Mr. Mulkerrin is a team player is a bit of an understatement. From the beginning, he really saw the sales activity as a team project. He was happy to share any tips that made his cold calls more successful, and very open to getting feedback from me and his team members when he was having trouble landing a new client.

Later, when Mr. Mulkerrin took over as District Sales Manager, he also stepped effortlessly into the role of mentor to the sales trainees. He regularly took the newest hires out with him on sales calls so that he could impart his concept of outstanding customer relations—the relationship-building that pays off with referrals. He supervised them in their first major sales assignments and debriefed them over lunch. He made sure they learned from every mistake, but never at the cost of their self-esteem. He also organized biannual weekend retreats for the sales staff, and maintained a friendly competition with other district managers. It took considerable coordination and dedication on Mr. Mulkerrin's part to guarantee his sales staff the support they needed. However, it was clear that he relished his leadership role.

This commitment bleeds over into his personal life and community involvement. He belongs to the Lions Club and sits on the board of the local Boys and Girls Club. Most recently, he began training to run the Portland Marathon. He also plays bass in a Bruce Springsteen cover band every Wednesday night. And believe it or not, he has picked up clients from several of these involvements. Don't get me wrong—his interest in these groups is genuine, not mercenary. He loves to run, he loves to jam, and he wants to take an active hand in shaping the after-school program where his children have benefited so much. But all of these are also intensely social occasions and the man apparently never misses an opportunity to sell.

The story that everybody tells around here is how, when Donal was snowed in at Milwaukee for an entire weekend, he ended up talking shop with business owners who were also stranded at the hotel and at the airport. Three new accounts resulted from the conversations Donal struck up at the airport. One was a doctor who referred his sister-in-law; another introduced us to a market that we had not previously explored. We still joke around the office about "the blizzard that keeps on giving."

When Mr. Mulkerrin announced last spring that he would be moving to Florida because his wife was starting business school, we were truly sorry to see him go. He would have had a very bright future here at Kappen; he was already being considered for another promotion. Although we wish him every success in his great new professional opportunities, I know I speak for the entire company when I say that Donal will be greatly missed at Kappen.

I can unreservedly recommend Donal Mulkerrin to you for any intermediate or senior sales or marketing position.

Sincerely,

Mazel, Natton & Oppenheimer
Stockton, CA

To Whom It May Concern:

I am writing to recommend Rosalva Drabble for the position of full-time state court interpreter employee for the Superior Court of Santa Clara County.

I am Of Counsel at Mazel, Natton & Oppenheimer, a criminal defense law firm; my practice focuses primarily on accident, malpractice and wrongful death claims. Our firm hires Rosalva Drabble on a contract basis when we deal with clients or material witnesses whose primary language is Spanish. Over the last year and a half, she has provided a total of 850 hours of service; more than half of that work has occurred in the last six months alone. Personally, I have employed Ms. Drabble's services on at least 14 cases—mainly on matters pertaining to the pretrial discovery phase; in sum, I have personally observed her performance for 50+ hours.

Her motivation for pursuing this profession had its genesis when she was called in for jury duty several years ago. As a fluent Spanish speaker, she was frustrated because she felt that the (non-certified) court-provided interpreter wasn't rendering certain phrases correctly for either the defendant or the plaintiff; however, the judge had instructed the jury to accept only the interpreter's words as testimony. She buttonholed the bailiff during a recess and asked him why the Spanish-speaking individuals in the case weren't being given proper linguistic representation. He referred her to the court clerk, who encouraged her to go through the certification process if she felt she could do better. Within a month, Rosalva earned the designation of Registered Interpreter by passing an English proficiency exam, registering with the Consortium for State Court Interpreters and taking its ethics course. To prepare for the rigorous certification exam, Rosalva also enrolled a one-year court interpreting program at Pace University's College of Extended Learning, which included courses on the legal system and extensive training in simultaneous interpretation.

Around that time, I ran into my old college roommate, Rob Drabble, who mentioned that his wife was looking to establish herself as an legal interpreter. I referred Rosalva to our HR director. Her performance interpreting for oral depositions was deemed excellent, and we began to use her services regularly.

The firm only hires court interpreters who have near-native fluency in both Spanish and English. Ms. Drabble's deep understanding of both the Latin and the American cultures has proven to be a valuable resource for face-to-face interpreting. Her broad knowledge of both Spanish and English enables her to interpret accurately for Spanish-speaking individuals from all walks of life—ranging from expert witnesses to street gang members. As a conversational speaker of Spanish, I can verify that she is very good at approximating the level of discourse used by the Spanish speaker for whom she is interpreting. And it goes without saying that we rely on her for complete confidentiality.

In an average month, Ms. Drabble may help our attorneys take several foreign, transnational, and domestic depositions and examinations under oath. Of the several interpreters that we contract with, all are very proficient at consecutive interpretation; however, Ms. Drabble's skill at simultaneous interpretation is superior to the others. Consequently, she is our preferred interpreter at arbitrations, court hearings and trials. On one or two occasions, when scheduling allowed, members of our firm have even worked around Ms. Drabble's availability. As a experienced court-certified interpreter and independent contractor, Ms. Drabble's language abilities are constantly in demand. She is "on call" for two other law firms; I surmise, however, that she requested our recommendation not only because we have employed her the most consistently, but because the diversity of the cases we take on provides her with the most challenging and stimulating working environment.

Our cases have given her ample opportunity to demonstrate extra-linguistic expertise and comportment as well. For example, because interpreters cannot allow their choice of words and tone to be influenced by their opinions, they must prevent themselves from reacting to graphic pictures or testimony. Last year, Rosalva interpreted for us on a case involving a pair of grisly killings. When the defendant was showed the photographs of the crime scene, Rosalva was also seeing them for the first time. She rendered the suspect's testimony in an impartial, unaffected way; afterwards, however, she confided to me she had found the photographs nauseating. This is by no means the only occasion where she has impressed us with her professionalism.

She is also committed to professional development. In addition to fulfilling all continuing education requirements, Ms. Drabble networks regularly with Spanish-language interpreters and translators of diverse national origins. The group, of which she is the informal leader, offers both social and professional benefits, as I had the opportunity to see for myself when my own social connection with Rosalva garnered me an invitation to one of their barbecues. Several members mentioned that this group allows them to enhance their linguistic skills by comparing regional and dialect-specific differences in slang and colloquial Spanish. Rosalva's personality is extremely pragmatic and pro-active, and it strikes me as very appropriate that she would be the fulcrum of such a valuable resource in her professional community.

I understand why she would prefer the stability of a full-time court interpreter position to her current situation as an independent contractor, but I nonetheless regret the prospect of losing Ms. Drabble's services. Your gain would be our loss. Highly skilled interpreters like her are hard to find. She has the language skills, the quickness of mind and the emotional poise to handle any interpreting situation that would arise in a courtroom environment. For all these reasons, I unreservedly recommend her for the position of full time court employee interpreter.

Sincerely,

Acix Energy Solutions

23 West St. Houston, TX 54321

I, Steve Best, hereby certify that I have personally known Hsiao-fei Hwang since August, 200x. I am a professional geologist in the state of Texas (License #5667) who has worked for 16 years in the field of petroleum engineering; in the last 5 years, I have specialized in reservoir simulation, secondary and tertiary recovery project analysis, economic project evaluation, and field development. I know of my own direct knowledge that the applicant for licensure has engaged in geological work for at least 4 of the last 5 years, as is required by the State of Utah. She has been employed as follows:

Associate Field Geologist, Acix Energy Solutions.
August, 200x–present.
Supervisor: Steve Best.

Hwang is responsible for petrophysical evaluation (processing and interpretation) of well log data for hydrocarbon evaluation of various operated and non-operated fields; she also performs volumetric reserves estimation (deterministic and probabilistic) by using REP (Reserve Evaluation Program) commercial software. Based on these geological and engineering data, and on her evaluation of the economic feasibility of new exploration blocks, she participates in field development and well planning, providing input on the location of perforation zones/new development wells.

Graduate Research Assistant, Petroleum Department, Bellman & Associates.
October, 200x–July, 200x.
Supervisor: Randall Cherny.

Hwang used Schlumberger's Eclipse simulation package to develop a reservoir simulator for tight gas reservoirs in the Lantos Basin, TX. She performed reservoir simulation to aid production forecasting and reserves estimation, as well as decision-making in developing future infill wells.

To the best of my knowledge, Hsiao-fei Hwang has never been convicted of an offense that has a direct bearing upon her ability to practice geology or geological engineering. I am not aware of any problems regarding this individual's mental health, nor any problems regarding her use of alcohol or prescription drugs which would interfere with the performance of her practice of the profession of geology. Neither am I aware of any complaints from either employer, nor any ethical problems which relate to geological practice. I know of no instances where the applicant was guilty of illegal conduct or professional misconduct. With regard to my knowledge of her prior compliance with all State and local laws and regulations governing the profession, I can verify that the applicant has functioned within acceptable standards of ethics and professional practice.

Having provided these personal assurances that Hsiao-fei Hwang satisfies the basic qualifications for licensure, I would now like to provide additional information that I believe could be useful to the Board in evaluating the applicant's potential to contribute to the profession of geology in the State of Utah.

I can affirm, in fact, that the applicant in question adheres to the highest standards of professional and ethical conduct. On the two occasions when Hwang has served as a technical witness (before the Oil and Gas Division of the Texas Railroad Commission), she provided accurate and honest testimony based solely on her technical expertise, and refused to express personal opinions or give speculative answers. She also declined to answer questions that pertained to engineering matters outside of her own field of competence. I understand that the professional geologist license in Utah is a general license; in my opinion the applicant does have the capacity and judgment to restrict geologic work to the area(s) in which she is competent.

Lastly, Hwang has more than once identified possible deleterious effects on air quality caused by the proposed spacing variance in infill well drills, which could consequently pose a danger to the safety of the workers in the field. On each of these occasions, she registered her concerns with her supervisors in an appropriate fashion.

I would appraise Hsiao-fei Hwang's skills in the relevant areas as follows:

Health, Environmental and Safety Regulations: EXCELLENT

Technical Competence: GOOD

Interpretation of Construction Contracts: GOOD

Project Administration: GOOD

Financing: GOOD

Scheduling: GOOD

Professional Integrity: EXCELLENT

Professional Reputation: EXCELLENT

Personal Integrity: EXCELLENT

I would entrust Hsiao-fei Hwang with responsibility for an important geologic project involving the life, property, health and welfare of the public.

On this 23rd day of January, 200x, I certify under penalty of perjury that the foregoing is true and correct.

Signature of Certifier
Texas Professional Geologist License #5667

TESTIMONIAL FOR A BUSINESS

Erin Davis
689 Wood Creek Road
Cleveland, OH 24245
(285) 555-8763
edavis@email.com

To Whom It May Concern:

As a satisfied customer, I am very happy to write this letter of reference for Duke Success Academy (DSA). I am very grateful to them for helping my daughter succeed on the SAT and in her AP Chemistry class, and I would recommend them to any parent who would like to bolster their child's performance and confidence—both for schoolwork and with standardized tests.

I had visited a few other college prep institutions, and ultimately I decided to enroll my daughter at Duke Success Academy because of three factors: the aura of professionalism, the track record of achievement by former students, and the customer service.

In essence, I felt like a valued customer from the moment I walked in. The owner of the company, Mr. Ralph Chalmers, answered all of my questions to my satisfaction, and his personal money-back guarantee that my child would be able to raise her test scores in two weeks gave me the confidence to do business with DSA. I liked the fact that the instructor/student ratio was low enough that my daughter would feel comfortable speaking up and asking questions. The office and classrooms were clean and well stocked with teaching materials, and the instructors carried themselves in a very professional manner. Despite dealing with many students and parents on a daily basis, the staff remembered me and greeted me by name. DSA has the resources and reputation of a large nation-wide company but the personable, attentive service of a family-owned franchise. From the comprehensive and insightful weekly reports that I received on my daughter's progress to the way I was thoughtfully offered tea whenever I waited in the reception area, I was continually impressed with Duke Success Academy's operations and philosophy of customer service.

Of course, none of this would matter if my daughter had not benefited academically from their services. We first enrolled Candace in the two-month intensive SAT prep course. The experience was so positive—not just from the perspective of academic improvement but also in terms of raising Candace's self-esteem about her ability to tackle a subject she had always struggled with. She raised her Math score from 580 to 760 on the diagnostic tests—and she eventually earned a 740 on that section of the actual test. Much of the credit goes to her instructors, Brian and Darcy, for creating a lively, fun learning environment, and demystifying problems and test-taking strategies. Candace assured me that her SAT instructors encouraged her to deal with setbacks in a very constructive way. On the eve of the test, she displayed a confidence that I had never seen her take towards any previous test-taking situation. And it was validated by her high score.

Later that year, when Candace's AP Chemistry teacher suggested that she seek out individual tutoring to raise her grade, we went back to DSA. In fact, Candace was the one who suggested that we contact Darcy Chu, her SAT Math instructor (and also a Chemistry graduate student), about one-on-one tutoring. Mr. Chalmers was happy to set up the meeting. Darcy sat down with me and Candace to discuss our goals and then wrote up a proposed tutoring plan for the seven weeks that remained before the AP test. At the time, Candace had a C– average in the class; we decided that we would aim to raise it at least to a solid B.

I really appreciated the weekly progress reports that Darcy provided me, because they showed me how she was trying to develop more effective study skills in my daughter and how I could best support her (for example, quizzing her on new mnemonic devices). Darcy's assistance positively impacted Candace in other ways as well. Because we had all agreed that Candace would bring a specific list of chemistry questions and problems to her tutoring sessions, she became more organized. She also stopped making careless mistakes on her homework and on quizzes. Candace's test and quiz scores improved from C–'s to B's very quickly, and then they climbed again a few weeks later to land consistently in the B+/A– range. By the time the AP test came along, Candace was doing so well with Darcy that a score of 4 seemed very realistic—and a 5 possibly within reach. Ultimately, she received a score of 4, which I consider a wonderful achievement considering that she was sick with the flu on the day of the test. With Darcy's help, Candace also managed to pull her grade up to a strong B+ in the class.

I have two younger children, who are in grade school; when the time comes that they need extra help preparing for standardized exams or getting an extra boost on their schoolwork, I will be entrusting them to the capable professionals at DSA.

Sincerely,

Benetti Shoes
114 Princeton Avenue #714 New York, NY 10304

To Whom It May Concern:

The undersigned is pleased to provide the following letter of reference for the firm of Zyzygy Solutions, Inc. We hired them earlier this year to manage our PIPEDA compliance processes, and they have met our expectations on every level.

Our company, Benetti Shoes, has sold fine footwear and handbags for 30 years; we developed an online presence about six years ago, but the e-commerce component really began to take off in the last two years. As online sales and revenue grew, it became increasingly clear that our potential growth was hampered by outdated software. Meanwhile, we were also aware that the latest amendments to the Personal Information Protection and Electronic Documents Act (PIPEDA), which affected us directly, were scheduled to go into effect in half a year's time. A corporate decision was made that the time had come to upgrade our security and privacy infrastructure.

Our intention all along was to comply not merely with the federal legislation but also with our customers' expectations; as a customer-driven enterprise, we wanted to assure our customers that the personal information they entrusted to us as part of the online retail experience would retain airtight confidentiality.

Our goals were: 1) to implement rules-compliant physical, organizational and technological controls to safeguard the collecting, storing and disposal of sensitive information; 2) to institute employee training to heighten awareness of the importance of maintaining the confidentiality of personal information.

Based in part on several strong referrals, we hired Zyzygy Solutions last August to help us develop a customer information security system that would comply with the newest anti-identity theft safeguard standards; such a program would necessarily include providing security and technology training for relevant employees in our company. Zyzygy was very familiar with PIPEDA, and it was very reassuring to work with a team that had a proven track record of helping companies reach compliance on this set of standards.

Zyzygy listened carefully to what we needed and the constraints under which we were operating, analyzed our processes and infrastructure, and produced a realistic plan for how to accomplish our objectives. They first conducted a comprehensive assessment of our internal and external communications systems and protocols. They also evaluated the hodgepodge of previous software solutions that had constituted our security controls to date, identified the salvageable functions and proposed workarounds for the pieces that were outdated but too deeply embedded in our business processes to eliminate outright.

The list of specific, prioritized recommendations that Zyzygy presented to us covered employee awareness training, physical security, Secure Socket Layer (SSL), controlling access, back-ups and storage of sensitive information, desktop security, passwords, anti-virus tools, software patches, email security, encryption, firewalls, Virtual Private Network security, remote access, and contingency planning. Zyzygy team leader William Tule deserves an especial mention for his extreme patience in explaining the technical aspects to our less tech-minded department managers. In the end, we chose to implement all but one or two of Zyzygy's recommendations. They proceeded to do so over the next week and a half, taking care to cause minimal disruptions to our daily operations.

After implementation, Zyzygy team members presented workshops on security and privacy issues and procedures—and not only for the sales and customer service representatives who deal directly with our customers' personal and financial data. They also provided training for the rest of the staff regarding the updated safeguards and security protocols they would be using to access network and email applications, both from our office computers and remotely. From what I saw, the Zyzygy presentations were very clear and appropriately geared to each department's level of potential security risk. Employees of various departments came away understanding how our technology had changed, how they were supposed to interact with it, and how this would provide an increased level of protection to our customers. In fact, several employees thanked management for instituting a systematic policy on protecting sensitive and proprietary information. (As noted, the security upgrade was originally intended to secure customer data, but as an added benefit, the new firewalls and encryption protocols protected our proprietary files as well).

Lastly, Zyzygy provided us with a written manual exhaustively documenting all the security controls and procedures. They also converted their training seminar outline into a short e-learning module; we will most assuredly be using that CD-ROM as a resource for troubleshooting security issues or for getting future employees up to speed on our new rules-compliant security and privacy programs and procedures.

Given our timeframe and limited resources for complying with PIPEDA, we were exceedingly pleased with the final results. Zyzygy demonstrated a clear understanding of our vision, schedule and budget requirements and showed extreme co-operation and flexibility in satisfying our needs. The services rendered by Zyzygy were to the entire satisfaction of Benetti management. I would recommend Zyzygy Solutions, Inc., without hesitation, to any owner for projects requiring IT consulting services. Please do not hesitate to contact the undersigned directly should you require additional information.

Sincerely,

Canyon State University
Asian Studies Dept.

To Whom It May Concern:

I fully support Summer Michaels' application for the year-long Education Abroad Program in Seoul, Korea. As her instructor for both semesters of Intermediate Korean, I can attest that she is linguistically equipped to undertake the coursework offered at Yonsei University. I believe that she is unusually prepared to make the most of her academic year abroad.

Summer managed a perfect attendance record in Korean 2A and 2B, and her work was uniformly excellent. She received the third highest grade point total in the class for both semesters.

Although Summer was one of the few non-heritage language learners in the class, she explained in one of her first oral presentations that her family history was entwined with that of South Korea; her grandfather had served as a U.S. military advisor to South Korea at Panmunjeom after the armistice, and her great-grandmother had taught at Ewha Womans University in Seoul during the 1920s. Perhaps because of this family exposure to Korean culture, Summer's pronunciation is quite good, with very little of the "American" inflections that hobble so many other non-native speakers. Of course, this could also be due entirely to her diligence. I understand that Summer also participates in an ongoing language exchange with an international student from Pusan. I have noted a distinct improvement in Summer's pronunciation over the last few months, and in fact, I would rate her accent as more precise than some of her Korean-American classmates.

As part of her final group project, Summer helped script and film a parody of the "K-horror" films that are so popular nowadays in Asia and as exports to the West. The resulting short film was topical, entertaining, and displayed a real appreciation of the colloquialisms of pop culture.

Summer's plans for her year abroad include continuing her Korean language studies, taking classes in her major, International Relations, and conducting interviews for an independent research project on the rising influence of multinational charities. I understand that Yonsei's International Study Office has recently increased the number of regular (Korean-language) university courses approved for students at the Advanced-Mid to Advanced-High level. If Summer continues at her current rate of progress, she should be ready to audit one of them by Spring semester.

The following is my evaluation of Summer's proficiency in Korean, as broken down into the four main linguistic skills:

Listening: Summer can follow the main idea and identify important details in oral discourse in moderately demanding contexts of language use (e.g., face-to-face formal and informal conversations, audiotapes and radio broadcasts) on relevant topics and at a slow to normal rate of speed. She understands a range of common vocabulary and a limited number of idioms.

Reading: Summer can follow main ideas, key words and important details in authentic prose from various text types (e.g., newspaper articles, educational content materials, stories, encyclopedia entries). She requires the use of a dictionary and may have to read several times for comprehension.

Speaking: Summer converses with confidence on routine tasks and social situations; she can communicate facts and ideas in moderate detail, demonstrating a range of everyday vocabulary, some common phrases and idioms. Grammatical structures are relatively basic, but errors are infrequent. Pronunciation is excellent.

Writing: Summer can confidently communicate everyday needs and requests; as far as academic writing goes, she has written several five-page compositions in Korean, expressing ideas of some complexity. The ambition of her ideas occasionally exceeds her syntactical repertoire, but overall, she demonstrates a very good control of simple structures, vocabulary, spelling and punctuation.

Summer Michaels has the maturity and social sensitivity to successfully adapt to a different environment and educational culture. I would rate her in the top 10% of all the Education Abroad Program applicants whose files I have helped evaluate this year. To reiterate, Summer Michaels has my strongest recommendation.

Sincerely,

Clarence Darrow
Junior High School

2114 Education Way Ellensburg, WA 12345

To Whom It May Concern:

As Principal of Clarence Darrow Junior High School, I am delighted to recommend a member of our trusted substitute teaching staff, Ms. Shana Mellish, for your teacher credentialing program. I have written letters of reference for fifteen or so individuals at a similar stage in their career; of that number, Shana Mellish is decidedly one of the most promising young teachers that I have encountered. She has fulfilled all of our stated expectations—and exceeded them.

Ms. Mellish currently holds an Emergency Substitute Teaching Permit for Prospective Teachers. Over the past eleven months, she has become one of our most popular and effective substitute instructors. She has filled in for several teachers in both 7th and 8th grade classes, and for a range of subjects, including Math, Social Studies, Language Arts and Spanish. In total, she has worked a total of 46 days at Darrow Junior High. Her longest substitution stint at our school involved teaching the 8th grade Honors Social Studies class for two weeks, when our regular teacher Alan Chen took sick leave last winter. The King County Unified School District operates a substitute teacher rating system, so that schools can request the highly rated teachers first. Because Ms. Mellish made a very good impression on us early on, Darrow teachers began to request her more and more often to substitute for them.

I have never seen this young woman present herself as anything but highly professional, both in dress and demeanor. According to all the teachers I have spoken to, Ms. Mellish always ably implemented the lesson plans that they had left for her, and her written reports summarizing classroom activities and student behavior were accurate and prompt.

I want to draw special attention to Ms. Mellish's excellent classroom control. The fact that Ms. Mellish is an Army Reservist who recently served a tour of duty in Iraq gave her an extra measure of respect from students who might otherwise have tried harder to test her limits. She has a warm teaching personality and wants to make learning come alive for the students; however, when she enforces order, she has a quiet, disciplined presence that brooks no nonsense. Once, I happened to pass by the study hall classroom after lunch period, I was taken aback by the silence from that normally boisterous classroom. When I looked in and saw that it was Ms. Mellish was supervising the room, I joked to her that Darrow Junior High should hire her exclusively to keep our students productive during study hall; I only regret that our annual budget would not allow us this luxury.

Ms. Mellish was able to leverage her unique life experience in other ways as well. Her written reports during her two-week stint as the Social Studies substitute indicate that whenever the class finished the assigned lesson plan early, she gave impromptu lectures on the geography and history of the Middle East.

The impact of these lessons even extended beyond the classroom. During our most recent parent-teacher conference night, Mrs. Donal, the mother of a seventh-grader, told me about the day that her son had come home very excited about what he had learned at school. He said that his Social Studies substitute teacher had made current events in the Middle East interesting for him; later that evening, they watched the evening news together and even discussed it afterwards. Mrs. Donal asked me to relay her sincere thanks to the substitute teacher who had inspired such interest.

Because Ms. Mellish has been so superbly reliable—and always such a welcome presence to the teacher's lounge—our staff will be very sorry to see her move on. However, she deserves to lead a classroom of her own. In my opinion, she possesses outstanding teaching instincts, and this is the right time for her to further develop them through the coursework and practicum of the teacher's credentialing program. I enthusiastically recommend her for your program.

Sincerely,

INDEX FOR
SAMPLE LETTERS OF RECOMMENDATION

INDEX OF SAMPLE LETTERS OF RECOMMENDATION

APPENDIX:
Application Requirements Regarding Letters of Recommendation

I had a student applying to grad school in Biology at University of Washington Seattle who wanted my LOR. Three days prior to the deadline for submitting the LOR, this student thought he'd try to "prod" me to complete the form. I of course had not yet sent the on-line LOR. We have the viewpoint that a letter on the deadline or a day after the deadline is generally above and beyond, perhaps even early. So my student, withdrew my name from the LOR reference list and then re-added my name, thinking this would cause their online application program to automatically belch another annoying email at me to request my LOR, thus reminding the feeble professor to sit down and get this important letter out. While his reasoning was sound, though annoying, the result was worse than he could have expected. The system would no longer allow me to submit a LOR which caused this fine young man fits in the middle of Finals week. He ultimately had to call U of W Admissions to straighten out the mess, so my LOR could finally be accepted.

– Dr. Twombly Vern
University of Pittsburgh

LAW SCHOOLS

	http://www.lsac.org/LSAC.asp?url=lsac/letters-of-recommendation.asp
Letter service?	The LSAC (Law School Admissions Council) provides a LOR service for pre-law students who have registered to apply through the LDSAS (Law School Data Assembly Service) web application. Use of LSAC's LOR service is optional unless a law school to which you are applying states that its use is required.
Number and type of LOR	LSAC will handle up to four general letters (LORs that are intended to be sent to every school to which you apply). Each recommender is permitted to submit one general letter and an unlimited number of targeted letters. A list of law schools and their LOR requirements (i.e., the number of letters recommended and accepted) can be found at www.lsac.org/LSAC.asp?url=lsac/letters-of-recommendation.asp, as well as a series of Flash demos about how to use the service to direct your general and targeted LORs. Moreover, LSAC offers a pull-down menu from which you can select the destinations for your letters; as you select each individual law school, a box showing that school's preferences for LORs will appear.
Accept committee LOR?	Policy varies by school. Check with the schools you plan to apply to.
When to submit LORs?	If you choose to use LSAC as your LOR clearinghouse, they will send your letters to law schools according to each school's specified schedule; i.e., some schools want LORs when the initial law school report is sent, some will take them when certain number of letters have been received, and so on. LSAC will send your general letters to law schools in the order in which they are received (up to the number required or preferred by the law school). If you opt to send your letters through campus or online letter services instead of LSAC, you should check with each law school as to when they would prefer to receive your LORs.
Notes	LSAC will accept copies of letters from undergraduate school credential services or career planning offices, but only if each letter is accompanied by a LSAC Letter of Recommendation form.

BUSINESS SCHOOLS

Letter service?	There is no standardized business school application service, and consequently, no centralized LOR service. You must arrange to have your letters forwarded directly to each business school; the easiest way to do this—and keep paperwork to a minimum for your recommenders—is to ask your mentors to write a single general letter that a campus or online LOR service will then take responsibility for copying and mailing to the appropriate institutions. In recent years, however, business schools have begun to require that recommenders submit their evaluations online as part of a web-enabled application. Most people find this a more time-consuming process; some have begun to limit the number of recommendations they are willing to offer.
Number and type of LOR	Requirements vary by school. Generally speaking, MBA programs require 2-3 letters.
Accept committee LOR?	Business schools are primarily interested in reviewing evaluations from employers and professional supervisors.
When to submit LORs?	Most MBA programs ask applicants to submit letters of recommendation at the same time that they submit the application. Note the instructions and deadlines of each individual institution.

ALLOPATHIC MEDICAL SCHOOLS

Letter service?	AMCAS (American Medical College Application Service) does not handle LORs. Most pre-med applicants choose to use a campus or online credential service to handle their LOR files.
Number and type of LOR	The minimum LOR requirement ranges from 2 to 6 recommendations, but most medical programs ask for 3 letters: 2 from science faculty + 1 from a non-science faculty member. Additional letters generally come from research or clinical mentors, health profession advisors, employers, and community service supervisors. Most schools will not accept character references, while a rare few require peer LORs. For an overview, see http://www.ltsc.ucsb.edu/health/info_sheets/med_school_letter_types.pdf.
Accept committee LOR?	Yes. One letter from a college or university pre-professional/pre-med committee is generally equivalent to three letters from faculty members (2 science and 1 non-science faculty). Most medical schools prefer that applicants who have access to a preprofessional committee make use of that service.
When to submit LORs?	When medical programs invite an applicant to submit a secondary (i.e., school-specific) application, they also request that LORs be sent at that time.

OSTEOPATHIC MEDICAL SCHOOLS

Letter service?	AACOMCAS (American Association of Colleges of Osteopathic Medicine Application Service) does not handle LORs. Letters should be sent directly to the medical schools from the recommenders (or via a campus or online credential service).
Number and type of LOR	Most schools require 1-2 academic letters, mainly from science faculty; some schools require an additional letter from a liberal arts professor. Nearly all osteopathic medical schools require applicants to include one letter from a physician; some merely prefer that the physician letter be written by a D.O., others state explicitly that they will not accept a letter from an M.D. Additional letters from research mentors, employers, and community service supervisors are generally welcome, though applicants should check to determine each school's policy. Review the LOR requirements for each medical school at http://www.aacom.org/colleges/index.asp or take a look at the summary here: http://www.greatlettersofrecommendation.com/osteopathicLORrequirements
Accept committee LOR?	Yes. One letter from a college or university pre-professional/pre-med committee is generally equivalent to three letters from faculty members (2 science and 1 non-science faculty). Most medical schools prefer that applicants who have access to a preprofessional committee make use of that service. Note that two schools (PCOM and PCOM-GA) do not accept individual faculty letters at all.
When to submit LORs?	Applicants should have their LORs sent to the individual schools when they are invited to submit a secondary (i.e., school-specific) application or supplementary materials.

DENTAL SCHOOLS

	https://aadsas.adea.org/aadsas2007/lor.html
Letter service?	The web application AADSAS (Associated American Dental Schools Application Service) also serves as the LOR clearinghouse for pre-dental students. AADSAS will copy the official letters submitted on behalf of the applicant and forward copies to the applicant's selected schools (i.e., AADSAS-participating institutions).
Number and type of LOR	Dental schools generally require 3 letters: 2 from science faculty + 1 from a health-care supervisor. When a 4th letter is required, it is usually from a non-science faculty. AADSAS will process all the letters of recommendation you choose to submit. For now, all letters of recommendation must be submitted in paper format.
Accept committee LOR?	Yes. The letter from a pre-health or pre-professional committee is usually equivalent to 3 faculty letters. If a Pre-Dental Committee Report is being submitted on your behalf, indicate the name of the individual submitting the letter or write "Pre-Dental Committee" when registering evaluators in AADSAS. You do not have to list individual evaluators whose letters are contained in or appended to your Pre-Dental Committee Report
When to submit LORs?	You may request that your letters be sent directly to AADSAS as soon as you have completed the AADSAS application. If you are applying to non-AADSAS schools, note the instructions and deadlines of each individual institution.
Notes	Some schools require additional letters of evaluation/recommendation aside from the letters submitted with the AADSAS application. To determine if your designated schools require letters from specific individuals (e.g., science profs, practicing dentists, etc.), check the "Participating Dental Schools" list on the AADSAS login page. (https://aadsas.adea.org/aadsas2007/supplemental/ins_designations_supp.htm)

OPTOMETRY SCHOOLS

	http://www.opted.org/info_links.cfm
Letter service?	Arrange to have your letters forwarded directly to each school of optometry.
Number and type of LOR	Requirements vary by school. Generally speaking, optometry schools require 2–3 letters; some merely ask that the letters be written by undergraduate faculty members familiar with the applicant's work; other schools specify letters from faculty members teaching natural science subjects (biology, chemistry, physics, mathematics). Check with each school to determine whether they require an additional reference from a supervising optometrist and/or accept letters from other health professionals.
Accept committee LOR?	Varies. At some schools, an evaluation submitted by a pre-professional committee is equivalent to three individual faculty members teaching natural science subjects. Some schools do not accept Committee Letters (one comprehensive letter) and/or letters written by a committee in lieu of three letters of recommendation that have been individually written.
When to submit LORs?	Request that your letters be sent when you complete the applications to each optometry school. At least one school strongly prefers self-managed applications (i.e., that all transcripts and Letters of Recommendation be included in the single application package/envelope that is mailed to the admissions office).

VETERINARY SCHOOLS

	http://www.aavmc.org/vmcas/evaluations.htm
Letter service?	eLOR stands for electronic Letters of Recommendation, a feature that was recently added to the VMCAS (Veterinary Medical College Application Service) web application to give applicants and evaluators the opportunity to complete the evaluation process over the Internet. Your evaluator only needs to complete one evaluation for you; VMCAS makes the needed copies that are sent to your designated colleges.
Number and type of LOR	Evaluation requirements vary by institution. Access the College Specifications page (http://www.aavmc.org/vmcas/college_requirement.htm) to determine the number and type of LORs required by your selected schools.
Accept committee LOR?	"Committee" evaluation letters and "composite" evaluation letters are accepted, as long as they are attached to a VMCAS evaluation form. At this time the eLOR system does not support committee or composite letters. However, when listing the committee/composite letter in the eLOR system, please refer to the committee chair or whomever signs the official VMCAS form.
When to submit LORs?	As long as you have registered your minimum three evaluators in the eLOR section, you will be allowed to submit your application before the evaluations have been submitted.
Notes	Your minimum three evaluators for eLOR can be any combination of paper or electronic form. School requirements, however, may vary. (For example: Colorado requires that all evaluations be electronic, indicating that paper recommendation mailings will slow down the processing of the application.) The VMCAS evaluation form is mandatory for all recommendations and all questions must be answered for the following colleges: Cornell, Colorado, Florida, Kansas, Michigan, Mississippi, Purdue, VA-MD, Wisconsin, Prince Edward Island.

PHYSICIAN ASSISTANT PROGRAMS

	https://portal.caspaonline.org/caspa2007/lor.html
Letter service?	The web application CASPA (Central Application Service for Physician Assistants) also serves as the LOR clearinghouse for pre-PA applicants. CASPA will copy the official letters submitted on behalf of the applicant and forward copies to the applicant's selected programs (i.e., CASPA-participating institutions).
Number and type of LOR	Physician Assistant graduate programs generally require 2–3 letters; the most often requested are LORs from science faculty or a pre-health advisory committee and health care professionals (preferably a PA). An applicant whose academic record has not been very strong may benefit by including an additional letter from a science professor.
Accept committee LOR?	Yes, CASPA will accept Committee Letters of Reference (in paper form only). A complete paper reference consists of the two-page CASPA Reference Request Form plus a letter submitted on the stationery of the individual writing the reference. If the Committee Letter of Reference is a compilation of several individuals and contains one Reference Request Form and one letter, it will be considered as one reference. The individual writing the reference will need to fill out the evaluation grid on the Reference Request Form. You will need to obtain two additional references. If you want the Committee Letter to count as more than one reference, you will need to have a Reference Request Form and a letter for each additional reference that will be in the Committee Letter packet. Each evaluation grid on the Reference Request Form will need to be completed by each individual. You should indicate each reference name in the Reference section of your application. Normally, these letters would be gathered by an advisor and sent together with a cover letter from the advisor.
When to submit LORs?	Have your letter writers submit your letters to CASPA once you have finished filling out the web application. If you are applying to non-CASPA schools, note the instructions and deadlines of each individual institution.

PHARMACY SCHOOLS

	http://www.pharmcas.org/applicants/eval.htm http://www.pharmcas.org/applicants/evalquestions
Letter service?	A few pharmacy schools prefer that applicants send references directly to the institution. Refer to individual school websites for details. PharmCAS will forward up to three references to all of your designated pharmacy schools, regardless of the school's preference. Evaluators may submit either electronic letters of reference (eLORs) or paper references to PharmCAS, but eLORs are preferred as paper references take longer to duplicate and send to the designated pharmacy schools.
Number and type of LOR	Pharmacy schools generally require 2–3 letters; the most often requested are LORs from science faculty and pharmacists. Review the PharmCAS School Reference Table (http://www.pharmcas.org/docs/ReqTypebySchool.pdf) to learn the number and types of evaluators required and not accepted by each institution. Do NOT send more than three (3) references to PharmCAS. Send any additional references directly to your designated pharmacy schools. Pharmacy schools may or may not consider extra references.
Accept committee LOR?	Yes, however, each of your designated pharmacy schools will decide whether a committee or composite letters may count as more than one reference. "Composite" letters typically represent a compilation of letters collected from various individuals. "Committee" letters generally represent a single letter with the collective thoughts of a group of designated individuals usually written by the chair or a designee. PharmCAS will accept the name of a college pre-health profession advisor in lieu of the evaluator(s).
When to submit LORs?	Once you complete the PharmCAS application, you may request that your letters to be sent directly to PharmCAS. They will begin to forward your references to your designated pharmacy schools once your file is complete (i.e., when they receive a reference from every evaluator that you listed). If you are applying to non-PharmCAS schools, note the instructions and deadlines of each individual institution.

About the Authors

Don Osborne is the President and Founder of INQUARTA, a leading graduate school admissions advising service specializing in MBA, medical, allied health, law and other graduate programs. INQUARTA (www.inquarta.com) is the largest private graduate school advising service in the United States and has served more than 2,000 students seeking acceptance to top grad school programs. Drawing on over 20 years of advising experience, Don has developed the MBA Success system, a multidimensional approach to application strategy.

Don is a popular speaker on college campuses and has given hundreds of seminars on graduate and professional school admissions. He has twice been invited to be a workshop speaker at the International Golden Key convention of 1,200 club officers and members from all over the world.

Prior to founding INQUARTA, Don was a member of The Princeton Review faculty, the co-author of The Princeton Review MCAT Verbal course, author of the Verbal Accelerator program, and a Teacher Trainer for MCAT Verbal, LSAT, and GMAT.

Lilly Chow has over twelve years of editing experience, which includes managing content for both print journalism and Internet sites. She graduated from the University of California, Irvine, with both a bachelor's and Master's Degree in Comparative Literature. Subsequently, Lilly helped develop web content for Qian Yang International, a media/film production company.

Since 1999, when she began working as Managing Editor at INQUARTA's Irvine office, Lilly has assisted more than 300 clients to articulate and express their dreams of pursuing graduate and professional education. In 2002, she opened a satellite office of INQUARTA in Northern California, where she served as Director and Head Counselor.

INQUARTA

The nation's leader in graduate school admissions advising

A graduate school advising program designed to make you as strong an applicant as you can be.

Founded in 1994, INQUARTA is the most respected private graduate school advising program in the United States. Our Integrated Counseling™ approach has been developed based on thousands of successful applicants to graduate school -- you have access to unparalleled experience.

INQUARTA is a one-on-one graduate school admissions advising, coaching and guidance program. Our success rate is built upon what works. We tell our students what they need to know and do, not just what they want to hear.

What does this mean to you?

We are committed to your successful admission to graduate school. We look at each student individually and develop a plan based on your strengths and weaknesses as a candidate. Our counselors then build a success plan around your strengths to make you a stronger applicant.

Why a Private Advisor... Why INQUARTA?

We will make you a stronger candidate than you can make yourself. We work with students who are concerned about how to overcome an average GPA, a test score that is not reflective of their potential, or students who have the grades but feel they might not have the "right stuff" graduate schools want to see in an application.

In 10 years, we have learned that...

Successful applicants are well-rounded, complete applicants. We believe that your application essays are developed over time, not written over a weekend; it takes time and thought to effectively express your experiences in your graduate school application.

How Can I Learn More about INQUARTA?

Got a question about getting into graduate school? Worried that your GPA isn't perfect, or that your scores are not high enough? Our counselors talk with students all over the country -- and we would be happy to talk with you. Call us at 800-987-3279 x. 211 and talk to an advisor, or email us at info@inquarta.com with your questions.

Call us at 1-800-987-3279 to schedule a Free Individual Consultation Session!

Outstanding Graduate School Applications for Medical, Dental, Optometry, Law, MBA and Other Programs
Get Ready. Get Prepared. Get Practice. Know What to Expect. Know What to Say. Know Your Stuff.

Visit us on the web at www.INQUARTA.com or email us at info@inquarta.com.

INQUARTA has simply mastered the fundamental principles of helping applicants get into grad school. Their thinking, program, approach and materials are without equal. I have never seen anything like it in my 20+ years of helping students reach for their educational goals.

—*Paul Kanarek, President and Co-Founder, The Princeton Reviews of Los Angeles, Orange County, Riverside and Washington DC*

INQUARTA

www.inquarta.com   800-987-3279 x. 211

Since 1994, INQUARTA has provided useful information, resources and advice regarding graduate school admissions and more. Our experience and strategies can be found in our books, planners and audios. Learn more at www.inquartashop.com.

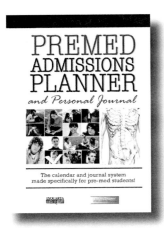

Pre-Med Admissions Planner
$19.95

This innovative four-year calendar is a must-have organizing tool for busy pre-medical students. If you want to make yourself more competitive for medical school, let this planner be your companion. Full of medical school admissions reminders, alerts, and deadlines, this one-of-a-kind planner can help you map out a pre-med experience that will make your medical school application shine.

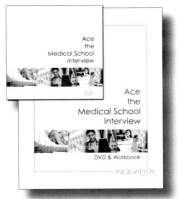

Ace The Medical School Interview DVD/Workbook
$29.95

Get an inside look into the medical school interview process with this DVD and workbook. The DVD includes a two-hour workshop and sample student interviews.

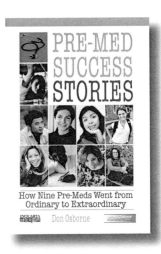

Pre-Med Success Stories
$24.95

PreMed Success Stories offers a multidimensional view of how a counseling team helped nine pre-meds package themselves for the medical school application process. This book is like sneaking a peek into the files of students you can relate to and sympathize with, complete with counselor's comments, editor's notes about the personal statement, and the advising team's recommendations on how to improve the student's chances for acceptance. These professional opinions are candid but non-judgmental, sometimes wry, and always full of encouragement.

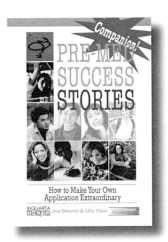

Pre-Med Success Stories Companion
$19.95

This companion workbook to *Pre-Med Success Stories: How Nine Pre-Meds Went from Ordinary to Extraordinary* features a practical, immediate way for readers to apply the lessons of the case studies to their own application process. In this workbook, you will find a set of action steps and writing prompts, each one inspired by a chapter of *Pre-Med Success Stories*, that invite you to reflect upon aspects of your own application with honesty and humor. Taken together, these exercises provide pre-meds with a valuable set of tools for embarking on their own application journey.

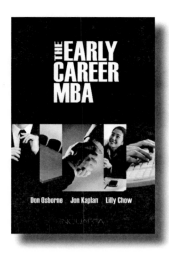

The Early Career MBA
$19.95

Early Career MBA is written for current or recent undergraduates who are considering applying to business school. This book will help you identify potential MBA programs that would be a good fit for you right out of college and then help you become as strong an applicant as possible for these business schools.

We also wrote *The Early Career MBA* for current undergraduate career counselors and pre-professional advisors. Here, for the first time, is a guide designed to help your students prepare for and learn how to take advantage of their MBA education once accepted.

Great Letters of Recommendation
$19.95

If you've ever felt anxious about the process of getting or writing a letter of recommendation, this book is for you! Packed with sample letters, templates, and advice, this guide is designed to help you distinguish between the run-of-the-mill "good" letter and the "great" letters that make admissions committees sit up and take notice.

Great Letters of Recommendation features 50 sample letters that run the gamut from high school to post-graduate, and from scholarship applications to work references and testimonials.

30 MCAT Verbal Passages
$29.95

Need more practice on the MCAT verbal section? Take on these challenging 30 passages developed by an MCAT verbal instructor with over 10 years experience teaching MCAT.

Save My GPA
$TBD

Coming soon! *Save My GPA* is a book of hundreds of study skill and time management tips to help you get better grades with less work. Check back with us as there is more to come.

Everybody loves **Free Stuff**. You will find tons of useful resources at our websites.

www.inquarta.com

Visit www.inquarta.com and look for pages of **free** content, .pdfs, video, and audio (coming soon!) to help the pre-med student.

Get a **free** sample chapter of *Pre-Med Admissions Planner and Personal Journal*, the only calendar system designed specifically for pre-med students.

Our Q-Cards are quick references to help you with many aspects of the med school application – personal statement, letters of recommendation, work/activities, school selection, secondaries, interviews. Check on our site for the **free** .pdfs.

www.premedsuccessstories.com

Download a **free** sample chapter of *Pre-Med Success Stories, How Nine Students Went from Ordinary to Extraordinary* at www.premedsuccessstories.com. *Pre-Med Success Stories* is a book of inspiring case studies that shows how nine pre-meds went through the entire application process and got in to med school. If they did it, you can do it too!

Pre-Med Success Stories Companion: How to Make Your Own Application Extraordinary. The exercises in the *Companion* will show you step-by-step how to make your own application as strong as possible. Get a **free** sample chapter of the *Companion* at www.premedsuccessstories.com.

www.lifehacksforcollege.com

Anything that solves an everyday proble in a clever or non-obvious way might be co a lifehack. The tips at www.lifehacksforcoll com are designed to solve the kind problems students have in college – ho deal with procrastination, organization time management. Come visit as we pro you with great **free** tools to improve college life.

www.savemygpa.com

Coming soon! SaveMyGPA is the home for hundreds of study skill and time management tips to help you get better grades with less work. Check on the site as we develop it this fall.

www.thenewmcat.com

Check out this website for all the latest news, tips and strategies about how to deal with the upcoming computer-based MCAT.

www.mcatverbal.com

Struggling with the verbal section of the M(Feel lost, overwhelmed, stuck? Tried every and nothing seems to work? Come to v mcatverbal.com for loads of tips and tric help you max out your verbal score. Best – it's **free**!

ORDERING FROM US IS EASY!

Order at our website www.inquartashop.com or call (1-800-987-3279 x. 211) or fax (1-949-863-9325).

Product Name	Price	Qty	Total

Sales Tax: Please add 7.75% for products shipped to California addresses.	Subtotal	
	CA add 7.75% Tax	
Shipping: U.S. orders will be charged current UPS ground shipping rates OR USPS media mail rate (with regards to weight and shipping distance). **Please specify shipping preference.**	Shipping **(Circle One)**	UPS
		USPS
	Total	

Payment

(Circle One)   AMEX   Visa   Master Card   Discover

Card Number_____

Name on card_____ Exp. Date_____

Billing Address

Name_____

Address_____

City_____ State_____ Zip____

Cell #_____

E-mail_____

www.inquartashop.com

We'd Love To Hear Your Feedback and Success Stories.

And let us know how we can best help you.

Call us at 949-417-1295 or email dono@inquarta.com

Thanks again for reading.

Don and Lilly

www.inquarta.com